Violence and Candidate Nomination in Africa

This comprehensive volume brings together a diverse set of scholars to analyze candidate nomination, intra-party democracy, and election violence in Africa. Through a combination of comparative studies and country-specific case studies spanning much of Sub-Saharan Africa, including Kenya, Zambia, and South Africa, the authors shed light on violence during candidate nomination processes within political parties. The book covers several cases that vary significantly in terms of democracy, party dominance and competitiveness, and the institutionalization and inclusiveness of candidate selection processes.

The authors investigate how common violence is during candidate nomination processes; whether the drivers of nomination violence are identical to those of general election violence; whether nomination violence can be avoided in high risk cases such as dominant party regimes with fierce intra-party competition for power; and which subnational locations are most likely to experience nomination violence.

Through its focus on violence in nomination processes, this book firmly places the role of political parties at the centre of the analysis of African election violence. While adding to our theoretical and empirical understanding of nomination violence, the book contributes to the literature on conflict, the literature on democratization and democratic consolidation, and the literature on African political parties.

This book was originally published as a special issue of *Democratization*.

Merete Bech Seeberg is Assistant Professor of Political Science at Aarhus University, Denmark, and affiliated with the CODE project on conflict and democratization. Her research centres on authoritarian elections, electoral manipulation and violence, and democratization. She is the author of *State Capacity, Economic Control, and Authoritarian Elections*.

Michael Wahman is Assistant Professor in the Department of Political Science at Michigan State University, USA. He specializes in democratization and elections in new democracies, particularly on the African continent. His earlier work is published in a wide range of journals including *Comparative Politics, Democratization, Electoral Studies, Journal of Peace Research*, and *Party Politics*.

Svend-Erik Skaaning is Professor of Political Science at Aarhus University, Denmark, and co-principal investigator of the Varieties of Democracy (V-Dem) project. His research interests include the conceptualization, measurement, and explanation of democracy and the rule of law. He has published numerous books and articles on these issues.

Democratization Special Issues

Series editors:
Jeffrey Haynes, London Metropolitan University, UK
Aurel Croissant, University of Heidelberg, Germany

The journal, *Democratization,* emerged in 1994, during 'the third wave of democracy', a period which saw democratic transformation of dozens of regimes around the world. Over the last decade or so, the journal has published a number of special issues as books, each of which has focused upon cutting edge issues linked to democratization. Collectively, they underline the capacity of democratization to induce debate, uncertainty, and perhaps progress towards better forms of politics, focused on the achievement of the democratic aspirations of men and women everywhere.

Recent titles in this series include:

Democracy Promotion and the Challenges of Illiberal Regional Powers
Edited by Nelli Babayan and Thomas Risse

Religiously Oriented Parties and Democratization
Edited by Luca Ozzano and Francesco Cavatorta

Religion and Political Change in the Modern World
Edited by Jeffrey Haynes

Political Opposition in Sub-Saharan Africa
Edited by Elliott Green, Johanna Söderström and Emil Uddhammar

Conflicting Objectives in Democracy Promotion
Do All Good Things Go Together?
Edited by Julia Leininger, Sonja Grimm and Tina Freyburg

From Bullets to Ballots
Edited by John Ishiyama

The Military's Impact on Democratic Development
Midwives or Gravediggers of Democracy?
Edited by David Kuehn

Authoritarian Diffusion and Cooperation
Interests vs. Ideology
Edited by André Bank and Kurt Weyland

Violence and Candidate Nomination in Africa
Edited by Merete Bech Seeberg, Michael Wahman and Svend-Erik Skaaning

For a full list of titles please visit
https://www.routledge.com/Democratization-Special-Issues/book-series/DEM

Violence and Candidate Nomination in Africa

Edited by
**Merete Bech Seeberg, Michael Wahman
and Svend-Erik Skaaning**

Routledge
Taylor & Francis Group

LONDON AND NEW YORK

First published 2019
by Routledge
2 Park Square, Milton Park, Abingdon, Oxon, OX14 4RN, UK

and by Routledge
52 Vanderbilt Avenue, New York, NY 10017, USA

First issued in paperback 2020

Routledge is an imprint of the Taylor & Francis Group, an informa business

British Library Cataloguing in Publication Data
A catalogue record for this book is available from the British Library

ISBN 13: 978-0-367-66379-7 (pbk)
ISBN 13: 978-0-367-14159-2 (hbk)

Typeset in Minion Pro
by RefineCatch Limited, Bungay, Suffolk

Publisher's Note
The publisher accepts responsibility for any inconsistencies that may have
arisen during the conversion of this book from journal articles to book chapters,
namely the possible inclusion of journal terminology.

Disclaimer
Every effort has been made to contact copyright holders for their permission to
reprint material in this book. The publishers would be grateful to hear from any
copyright holder who is not here acknowledged and will undertake to rectify
any errors or omissions in future editions of this book.

Contents

Citation Information

The chapters in this book were originally published in *Democratization*, volume 25, issue 6 (September 2018). When citing this material, please use the original page numbering for each article, as follows:

Chapter 1
Candidate nomination, intra-party democracy, and election violence in Africa
Merete Bech Seeberg, Michael Wahman and Svend-Erik Skaaning
Democratization, volume 25, issue 6 (September 2018), pp. 959–977

Chapter 2
Battleground: candidate selection and violence in Africa's dominant political parties
Shane Mac Giollabhui
Democratization, volume 25, issue 6 (September 2018), pp. 978–995

Chapter 3
Fighting for a name on the ballot: constituency-level analysis of nomination violence in Zambia
Edward Goldring and Michael Wahman
Democratization, volume 25, issue 6 (September 2018), pp. 996–1015

Chapter 4
Electoral violence during party primaries in Kenya
Fredrick O. Wanyama and Jørgen Elklit
Democratization, volume 25, issue 6 (September 2018), pp. 1016–1032

Chapter 5
Fighting your friends? A study of intra-party violence in sub-Saharan Africa
Bryce W. Reeder and Merete Bech Seeberg
Democratization, volume 25, issue 6 (September 2018), pp. 1033–1051

Chapter 6
The Party Paradox: a Comment Nicolas van de Walle (Cornell) February 20, 2018
Nicolas van de Walle
Democratization, volume 25, issue 6 (September 2018), pp. 1052–1062

For any permission-related enquiries please visit:
http://www.tandfonline.com/page/help/permissions

Notes on Contributors

Jørgen Elklit is Professor of Political Science at Aarhus University, Denmark. His professional interests include elections and electoral systems, political parties, and democratization. He has also been an election and democratization advisor in Africa, Europe, and Asia. In 2008 he served as Secretary to the Independent Review Commission in Kenya.

Edward Goldring is a PhD student in the Department of Political Science at the University of Missouri, USA. His research focuses on how non-democratic regimes and leaders maintain power. His work has been published in journals including *Democratization* and *Africa Spectrum*.

Shane Mac Giollabhui is a Lecturer at the School of Applied and Social Sciences, University of Ulster, Northern Ireland. His research on political parties and the police has appeared in *African Affairs*, *Party Politics*, *The British Journal of Criminology*, and *Qualitative Research*.

Bryce W. Reeder is Assistant Professor of Political Science at the University of Missouri, USA, and an affiliate of the Truman School of Public Affairs. His research centres on political violence, conflict management, and the consequences of wars for civilian populations.

Merete Bech Seeberg is Assistant Professor of Political Science at Aarhus University, Denmark, and affiliated with the CODE project on conflict and democratization. Her research centres on authoritarian elections, electoral manipulation and violence, and democratization. She is the author of *State Capacity, Economic Control, and Authoritarian Elections*.

Svend-Erik Skaaning is Professor of Political Science at Aarhus University, Denmark, and co-principal investigator of the Varieties of Democracy (V-Dem) project. His research interests include the conceptualization, measurement, and explanation of democracy and the rule of law. He has published numerous books and articles on these issues.

Nicolas van de Walle is the Maxwell Upson Professor of Comparative Politics at Cornell University, USA. He has published widely on democratization issues as well as on the politics of economic reform and on the effectiveness of foreign aid, with special focus on Africa.

Michael Wahman is Assistant Professor in the Department of Political Science at Michigan State University, USA. He specializes in democratization and elections in new democracies, particularly on the African continent. His earlier work is published in a wide range of journals including *Comparative Politics, Democratization, Electoral Studies, Journal of Peace Research,* and *Party Politics.*

Fredrick O. Wanyama is Deputy Vice-Chancellor, Academic and Student Affairs at Kisii University, Kenya, and Associate Professor of Political Science at Maseno University, Kenya, where he earned his PhD in Political Science. His research interests are in comparative and development politics. He is widely published within these fields in books, journals, and encyclopaedia.

Candidate nomination, intra-party democracy, and election violence in Africa

Merete Bech Seeberg, Michael Wahman and Svend-Erik Skaaning

ABSTRACT
This article introduces a special issue on candidate nomination, intra-party democracy, and election violence in Africa. Although a burgeoning literature on African democratization has focused on the topic of electoral violence, little attention has been given to violence during party nominations. When local-level or national-level competition between parties is low, as in much of Africa, electoral politics become a matter of intra-party rather than inter-party competition. Nominations are a part of the electoral process often left to the discretion of poorly institutionalized parties, free of the involvement of electoral management bodies and external monitors, and violence often results. Rather than developing an elaborate theoretical framework on the causes of nomination violence, our ambition in this introduction is to introduce the concept of nomination violence and situate it in the literatures on intra-party democracy and election violence. We also offer new descriptive data on nomination rules and nomination violence across parties on the African continent. The data show that nomination violence is a prevalent problem across both democracies and electoral autocracies. However, the level of nomination violence varies significantly between parties in the same party system and we recommend further research into the effect of parties' selection procedures on nomination violence.

Two and half decades after the broad reintroduction of African multi-partyism, research on African elections has matured significantly. Scholars of contemporary democratization have devoted much energy to uncovering the dynamics of inter-party competition, noting how the weakness of political opposition has affected the prospects for real competition and democratic consolidation.[1] Others have emphasized how persistently high levels of manipulation have rendered many African elections democratically inadequate,[2] and how authoritarian regimes' violent repression has increased during periods of intense electoral competition.[3] Democratization scholars have concluded that most of Africa has not yet transitioned to electoral democracy; a majority of the formally democratic African states are best described as electoral autocracies.[4]

When inter-party competition is low, nationally or locally, electoral politics becomes a matter of intra-party, rather than inter-party, struggle. Whereas much research on the African one-party state revolved around the internal organization and functioning of African ruling parties,[5] conspicuously little is known about intra-party politics after the introduction of multiparty elections. Absent inter-party competition, local and national elites continue to compete for power within locally or nationally dominant parties.[6] However – just as in much of the Western world – candidate nomination has remained "the secret garden of politics",[7] and scholars of democratization have just started to acknowledge the potentially crucial importance of such intra-party contests for the further development of democracy.

Candidate nomination is a process often left to the discretion of poorly institutionalized parties, free from the involvement of election management bodies and out of sight of international election monitors. However, when nomination procedures fail to meet acceptable democratic standards, the democratic chain of electoral politics is broken even before the onset of inter-party competition. Given the high stakes involved in candidate nomination, it is hardly surprising that candidate nomination processes in the African multiparty state have often turned violent.[8] However, the emerging literature on electoral violence has hardly touched upon the topic of nomination violence.

In this special issue, we bring together a diverse set of scholars to theorize and analyse nomination violence on the African continent. The contributors ask a range of questions that have not been answered by the literatures on political parties and election violence: How common is violence during candidate nomination processes? Are the drivers of nomination violence identical to those of general election violence? Can nomination violence be avoided in high risk cases such as dominant party regimes with fierce intra-party competition for power? What subnational locations are most likely to experience nomination violence? While adding to our theoretical and empirical understanding of nomination violence, the issue aims to contribute to the literature on conflict, the literature on democratization and democratic consolidation, and the literature on African political parties.

Elklit and Wanyama explore the causes of nomination violence in a qualitative study of some of the most recent candidate nomination processes in multi-party Kenya. They argue that Kenyan parties have been characterized by organizational weakness and have not been able to regulate intense competition for nomination for ethno-regional dominant parties that guarantee nominees to win seats in their strongholds, resulting in outbursts of nomination violence. Goldring and Wahman explore the same processes in multi-party Zambia but rely on sub-national, statistical data. They find, among other things, that districts with a clear front-runner, proxied by a sitting MP running for re-election, are much less likely to see nomination violence, indicating that nomination violence is related to high levels of intra-party competition.

In a cross-national as well as sub-national comparative study, Reeder and Seeberg explore the relationship between inter-party competition and violence. They ask whether the timing and causes of intra-party violence (including but not restricted to nomination violence) differ from that of general election violence. They find that whereas general election violence is common both during the election campaign and in the electoral aftermath, intra-party violence primarily occurs prior to elections. Furthermore, the risk of intra-party violence, unlike general election violence, increases as inter-party competition decreases, making intra-party violence more common in districts where a single party dominates.

Finally, Mac Giollabhuí argues, based on the case of the African National Congress (ANC) in South Africa, that political dominance does not necessarily lead to large-scale nomination violence. Mac Giollabhuí shows that ANC leaders in the early development of the party perceived high risks of intra-party violence due to the ANC's political dominance and the social and ideological diversity within the party. However, through the adoption of closed-list PR in combination with investment in an organization that can impartially follow the rules set out for nomination processes, intra-party violence within the party has remained limited.

The purpose of this introductory article is not to formulate and test theories on the causes of nomination violence. Rather, we aim to point to the importance of studying intra-party violence and to theoretically and empirically contextualize the independent contributions in the special issue. First, we situate the topic of the special issue in relation to two different research traditions: the literature on intra-party democracy in developed as well as developing countries and the recent literature on electoral violence. We believe that these literatures have to be understood in tandem to address the problem of nomination violence adequately. Second, we clarify the central concepts of nomination violence and candidate nomination procedures. Third, we argue that we have little cross-national data on the organization of candidate nomination or violence in the major political parties across the globe and make a first attempt at collecting such data through an expert survey of intra-party dynamics in Sub-Saharan Africa. Fourth, we use the data to gain insight into processes of candidate nomination in parties that are often new or changing. We argue that variations in such processes could be a hitherto unexplored driver of nomination violence and should be a topic for future studies.

The empirical overview also allows us to place some of the more case-specific processes illustrated in the individual papers in a more continent-wide perspective. Looking at party-level assessments of nomination violence we see significant variations in the level of nomination violence between countries but also between parties in the same country. This finding adds to an emerging realization among scholars of African politics that African parties, even within the same party systems, tend to vary significantly in their organizations and operations.[9]

The literatures on election violence and candidate nominations

The literature on election violence has matured significantly in recent years. Whereas conflict scholars have acknowledged how elections represent a focal point that may change levels of conflict and repression,[10] democratization scholars have concentrated on how violence affects the electoral process. There is an emerging consensus that violence should be considered a form of manipulation[11] that distorts the quality of elections.[12] Violence is generally seen as a socially unacceptable practice with the potential of reducing perceived levels of electoral legitimacy.[13] Sub-Saharan Africa – being the world region with the highest number of electoral autocracies[14] and with several countries recently emerging from civil conflict – is the context where most work on election violence has been conducted. Nonetheless, most existing work on election violence has paid no or little attention to election violence occurring in connection to candidate nomination processes. In the emerging literature on African nominations, money and corruption have been documented to play a significant part in the distribution of power within African parties,[15] but violence is much less studied than money as a political tool for gaining power.[16]

We argue that this neglect is problematic for two reasons. First, the effects of nomination violence are likely to be as detrimental – both in terms of human suffering and in undermining democratic quality – as those of general election violence occurring across party lines. Second, the dynamics and causes of nomination violence are likely to be different from those of inter-party election violence. Previous studies have highlighted a plethora of factors that shape the risk of electoral violence, including natural resource wealth, prior or ongoing conflicts,[17] whether the country is democratic, levels of state capacity,[18] the type of electoral system,[19] and characteristics of the race, including the stakes (e.g. whether presidential or parliamentary power is up for grabs) and the level of competitiveness.[20]

Although we may reasonably expect that several factors will be associated with an enhanced risk of both general election violence and nomination violence, there are also important differences in how one might theorize general election violence and nomination violence. First, nomination violence is to a high extent of an intra-party rather than inter-party character. Intra-party violence – more often than general election violence – may be of an intra-ethnic character. Second, the selectorate, although variable (depending on rules for nomination), is usually smaller in party nominations than general elections, affecting the potential targets of nomination violence. Third, nominations are temporally removed from the general election and may not shape general election behaviour to the same extent as violence happening shortly before elections.

One factor very likely to affect nomination violence but unrelated to levels of general election violence is the organization of individual parties. In particular, procedures for nominating candidates for elections are likely to affect the risk of violence during the process. The existing literature on intra-party democracy primarily focuses on how candidate nomination rules affect democratic quality by determining the representation of specific groups in parliament.[21] Furthermore, it has mainly discussed Western democracies.[22] This has meant that the potential relationship between intra-party democracy and the risk of violence has been neglected. Tellingly, the most elaborate book hitherto on candidate nomination methods and their consequences does not mention violence at all.[23]

This special issue contains accounts of party nominations in widely different settings. Some regimes are more democratic, such as South Africa, others are more autocratic, such as Zimbabwe and Uganda. Some party systems are nationally competitive, like Zambia and Kenya, others are more dominant, like Uganda and South Africa.[24] Much research has dealt with the concept of party institutionalization. Party institutionalization is a complex and multidimensional concept. Here we will pay particular attribute to one specific dimension of party institutionalization, the institutionalization of rules in relation to candidate nomination.[25] That is, to what extent are rules for candidate nomination known and respected within the party organization.

The special issue covers several cases that vary significantly in terms of democracy (e.g. Reeder and Seeberg in this issue), party dominance and competitiveness (e.g. Goldring and Wahman; Reeder and Seeberg, and Mac Giollabhui in this issue), and the institutionalization and inclusiveness of candidate selection processes (e.g. Elklit and Wanyama; Mac Giollabhui in this issue). For the purpose of the introductory article, we first clarify the concepts of nominations and violence. We then move on to empirically assess differences in nomination procedures and violence across parties and party systems in Sub-Saharan Africa.

4

Election violence, intra-party violence, and nomination violence

In this study, we are interested in a particular subtype of violence that occurs in relation to processes of candidate selection within parties prior to elections. Nomination violence, as we call it, is a subtype of two other – partly overlapping – types of political violence: election violence and intra-party violence (see Figure 1).

According to Höglund,[26]

> electoral violence is separated from other forms of political violence by a combination of timing and motive. The time aspect relates to violence carried out during the election period. The objective of electoral violence is to influence the electoral process and in extension its outcome.

Intra-party violence is primarily defined by the actors involved as well as the motive: It is violence that occurs between supporters, members, or candidates of the same party and relates to the party's internal policies. Both election violence and intra-party violence are subtypes of political violence. Although distinct, they also overlap.

It is at this intersection of intra-party violence and election violence that we find nomination violence (see Figure 1). Definitions of electoral violence typically distinguish between different actors, activities, timing, and motives. These distinctions can also be applied to nomination violence.

In terms of *motives*, nomination violence relates specifically to the candidate selection procedure in a political party as it is aimed at affecting the selection process or, alternatively, it arises out of frustration with the process. Goldring and Wahman (in this issue) make the distinction between horizontal and vertical nomination violence. Horizontal violence is conducted between rivalling candidates or their supporters to affect the outcome. Here, the victims are often members of the selectorate, rivalling candidates or her supporters. The perpetrators are typically allies or agents of opposing candidates. Vertical violence is conducted by local candidates and their supporters and directed towards national party organizations or the state itself. This form of violence may arise as a result of an unwelcome outcome that the loser or her supporters seek to overturn. For instance, in the All Progressive Congress (APC) primaries for the 2017 council polls in Lagos state, Nigeria, violence was directed towards the

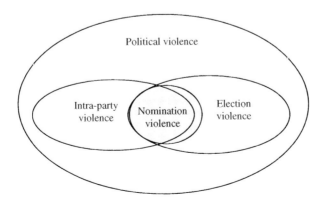

Figure 1. Types of violence.
Note: The grey-shaded oval indicates nomination violence.

Chairman of the APC elections committee. Local party supporters accused the national party of imposing candidates that were not locally supported.[27]

In terms of *actors*, nomination violence is most likely to occur between supporters, members, and/or candidates of the same party. In theory, however, supporters of other parties could also interfere violently with a given party's selection process. Thus, nomination violence is not a full subset of intra-party violence in Figure 1 as some nomination violence may occur across parties However, the great likelihood that both perpetrators and victims of violence belong to the same party is a characteristic that distinguishes nomination violence from general election violence (see Wanyama and Elklit in this issue).

With regards to *timing*, the period for candidate selection will depend on the procedures applying to the given party (see below). As for election violence, it seems useful to distinguish between three phases: An initial phase where the selectorate considers whom to vote for or appoint; the actual polling or selection; and the concluding phase where votes are counted, and the results are declared. Nomination violence can occur in all three phases, although nomination violence is also temporally distinct from general election violence as it occurs prior to the electoral campaign where inter-party electoral competition takes place.

Finally, the *activities* included in our definition of nomination violence are physical harm against people or their property as well as the threat of such physical harm. We include threats of violence in the definition as these have often turned out to be critical during electoral processes. For instance, the 2013 elections in Zimbabwe were relatively peaceful compared to the 2008 campaign, at least fewer deaths and outright acts of physical violence were recorded. However, the ruling ZANU-PF's victory is commonly thought to have depended on a "dividend of fear" where subtle threats along with a history of electoral violence were sufficient to affect voting behaviour and opposition campaigns.[28,29]

Against this backdrop, and inspired by Sisk's[30] definition of electoral violence, we define nomination violence as acts or threats of physical harm against persons or property related to candidate selection processes within political parties. In principle, such violence may occur between parties, but most commonly, it takes place between candidates, members, or supporters of the same party. Hence, this intra-party nomination violence (the shaded oval in Figure 1) is the centre of attention of the majority of studies in this special issue.

Candidate selection processes

Candidate nominations are the process by which political parties choose who will be their recommended candidates for a particular election, such as national presidential or parliamentary elections.[31] Candidate selection methods are expected to influence political behaviour in general,[32] and this is likely to include the risk of political violence. They have been described as: "The most vital and hotly contested factional disputes in any party … for what is at stake in such a struggle … is nothing less than control of the core of what the party stands for and does."[33] Just as electoral systems affect the risk of social and political conflict,[34] candidate selection procedures determine how political power is achieved as they regulate a necessary step towards attaining elected office in political systems dominated by political parties rather than independent candidates.

Parties select candidates in many different ways. The process is occasionally regulated in detail by national law, but mostly the law (if any) merely and vaguely states that the selection process must be democratic. This means that in most cases the decision is largely determined by the party's internal rules. Hence, we find a lot of variation both across countries and across parties within the same country. Within parties, we also frequently witness changes as candidate selection procedures are typically less stable than national political institutions such as electoral systems.[35]

Parties' candidate selection procedures are typically categorized along four dimensions.[36] First, who can be selected? Formal regulations normally request candidates to be party members and maybe add some additional criteria about having serviced the party, local residence, or other things considered to be important by the party organization. Second, who is member of the selectorate? Normally the selectorate falls within three broadly defined groups: all party members, a broad share of selected party member delegates, or a narrow group consisting of, or appointed by, the party leadership. Third, how centralized is the process? The candidate selection may take place either at the national, regional, or local level. Fourth, what is the method of selection? Candidates may be selected either by voting or by appointment.

Three of the four dimensions are mutually dependent. For example, if the party leadership decides that the selectorate is narrow, the process is centralized, and the candidate selection will normally be a matter of appointment. When we present our newly collected data below, we have therefore collapsed information on the selectorate, centralization, and selection method and termed it "inclusiveness". Furthermore, interesting variation in candidate selection procedures are not fully captured by these four dimensions. Thus, we suggest a fifth dimension, for which we also collect data, namely, the degree of institutionalization of the process. Candidate selection may follow formal procedures written down in party regulations, the procedures may be unwritten yet well-known or established, or they may be more fluid to the degree where they simply consist of "discussions in 'smoke-filled rooms'".[37] Some party leaders attempt to avoid formalization of rules to uphold candidate selection procedures as patronage-based races over which they have ultimate control.

Data on candidate selection procedures and nomination violence

A prominent problem for scholars interested in nomination violence is a severe lack of data.[38]

Although studies of candidate nominations outside the Western world have emerged,[39] most systematic data on candidate selection procedures is only available for single countries in the developing world. No comprehensive dataset exists on procedures for nomination in African parties.

Similarly, we lack detailed data of intra-party violent events within countries and over time (see Reeder and Seeberg in this issue), but we also lack simple descriptive data across the continent. Lack of data is problematic for quantitative studies on nomination violence. Equally important, the lack of cross-national data affects our ability to situate more case-specific qualitative work in a wider context. Giollabhuí (in this issue) makes an argument for more inclusive nomination procedures, but what variation in inclusiveness do we have across the African continent? Wanyama and Elklit (in this issue) argue that the lack of institutionalized rules for nominations in Kenya was conducive to nomination violence, but how typical is this lack of institutionalization for the

African continent more broadly? Reeder and Seeberg (this issue) show that nomination violence is more common in districts where a party dominates elections. But how do African dominant parties such as NRM in Uganda, CCM in Tanzania, ZANU-PF in Zimbabwe, and ANC in South Africa compare in their propensity to experience nomination violence?

We here present new data on candidate selection procedures and violence in Africa in an attempt to establish an empirical benchmark. The data are based on surveys of 86 experts conducted in July–November 2016. We sent surveys to several local and international experts for every multiparty state (understood as any state where parties are allowed and where candidates from more than one party won representation in parliament[40]) with more than one million inhabitants. The data we have collected cover information on 64 parties in 25 countries[41] and focus on nominations for parliament in the most recent election prior to the fall of 2016.[42] It is important to note that this is not a full sample of Sub-Saharan Africa, since a total of 41 countries fit the description above. Smaller countries, where fewer social scientists conduct research on elections and countries with particularly low levels of democracy and effectively irrelevant elections are particularly missing from the sample. Nevertheless, our partial sample exhibits important variations across the dimensions discussed above. The sample includes democracies, such as South Africa and Ghana, as well as electoral authoritarian regimes with differing degrees of competitiveness ranging from more competitive regimes like Zambia to more dominant party regimes such as Ethiopia and Uganda.[43] For each question, the sample reflects the countries where we received replies from at least one expert. The data collection partly took place in connection to Anaïd Flesken's expert survey on Party–Citizen Linkages,[44] which covered fourteen Sub-Saharan African countries, and partly through a separate effort in which only our own questions were included.[45]

An important feature of the survey is that parties, rather than countries, are the unit of analysis. The identified expert is asked to answer the questions separately for each major party. This sets the survey apart from other new datasets, such as Varieties of Democracy[46] and Perceptions of Electoral Integrity,[47] which offer indicators on cross-national variations in nomination processes and/or violence. An emerging consensus among scholars of African party politics is that researchers ought to study parties rather than party systems. Parties, even within the same party system, vary significantly.[48]

The collected data tap into two issues: candidate nomination procedures and violence in relation to such nominations. In relation to nominations, our first question asks about the size of the selectorate, ranging from all voters, over ordinary party members, selected party delegates, to non-selected party elites, and the party leader.[49] It also enquires into the selection method. More specifically, our survey question asks: "Which of the following options best describes who has more power regarding the selection of candidates for the national legislative election (if practices differ across districts, please refer to the most common practice)?" The response categories are: (i) All voters through primaries, caucuses, mail ballots, or the like; (ii) Party members and or other party supporters through primaries, caucuses, mail ballots, or the like; (iii) Party members only through primaries, caucuses, mail ballots, or the like; (iv) Party delegates through conventions, central committees, congresses, or delegate bodies especially selected for the purpose of selecting candidates; (v) Both party elite/leader and party delegates/members/supporters influence the selection process through a relatively balanced bargaining; (vi) Party elites (small party agencies and committees that were indirectly selected or other less formal groupings); (vii) Party leader. With this question, we not only get information on the selectorate and selection method, but also automatically achieve information on the degree of centralization.

Second, we find it particularly relevant in an African context to shed light on the institutionalization of the nomination process.[50] Therefore, we pose an additional question aimed at assessing how institutionalized the candidate selection process is: "Which of the following options best describes the rules for the selection of candidates for the legislative election?" The response categories are: (i) Candidate selection follows clear rules written down in party regulations or national law; (ii) Candidate selection follows clear rules, which are, however, not written; (iii) There are clear rules for candidate selection, but these are often disregarded by the party leadership; (iv) There are clear rules for candidate selection, but these are often disregarded at the local level; (v) Candidate selection procedures are informal and unclear.

Lastly, to get to the actual level of violence, we ask experts the following question: "In the most recent candidate selection process for the national legislative election was the selection period free from violence between members or supporters of this party?" Response categories are: (i) There were no acts of physical violence and no threats; (ii) There were no acts of physical violence but some threats; (iii) There were only a few acts of physical violence. There were no deaths, but a few were injured; (iv) There were many acts of physical violence including injuries and threats but no deaths; (v) There were some acts of physical violence. They resulted in less than 10 people dead; (vi) There were many acts of physical violence. They resulted in more than 10 people dead; (vii) There were many acts of physical violence. They resulted in more than 100 people dead. These estimates are best understood as approximations. It is impossible to verify that experts have a precise estimation of the extent of violence in party nomination. However, these approximations serve as a rough first estimate on the problem of nomination violence in Sub-Saharan Africa.

Variations in rules for party nominations and nomination violence in Africa

We use the new dataset to establish a descriptive, empirical benchmark for the individual contributions in the special issue. Figure 2 shows the level of inclusiveness in the nomination process for the 64 parties in our sample.[51,52] The data indicates the presence of important variation in the procedures used for candidate nomination. A majority consisting of 71% of the parties in the sample has decentralized nomination for parliamentary candidates, meaning that national party leaders or party elites do not solely decide candidate nomination. In 55% of the parties, delegates are involved in the process. Only 16% of the parties decide nominations by primaries where either party members or voters are involved. The distinction between primaries permitting non-members and those reserved for existing party members is probably less relevant for most African parties than in for instance Western European parties. As the Kenyan case shows (Wanyama and Elklit in this issue) party membership is often an elusive concept in the African context where most parties lack a stable membership register and most citizens are unlikely to pay membership dues.

The size of the selectorate and the degree of decentralization will have consequences for the level of control that national and local elites maintain throughout the process. It

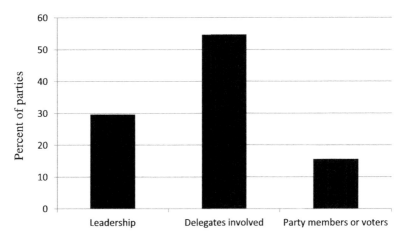

Figure 2. Inclusiveness of parliamentary candidate nominations across Sub-Saharan African parties.

Note: Percentage of parties displaying different degrees of inclusiveness in candidate selection. "Leadership" indicates that candidates are selected by the party leader or party elites. "Delegates involved" indicates that delegates are involved in selecting candidates either alone or along with the party leadership. "Party members or voters" indicates candidates are selected by party members, supporters, and/or all voters regardless of the method for selection. The data relate to the latest parliamentary election prior to the fall of 2016.

may also have repercussions for the incentives to engage in localized violence – a topic discussed by several contributions to the special issue (Elklit and Wanyama; Mac Giollabhuí). Some parties, as the case of Zambia illustrates (see Goldring and Wahman in this issue), employ hybrid forms of nomination where local party representatives are consulted to rank available candidates, but national elites make the final decisions. However, even in systems where significant powers are delegated from national or local party elites, such elites may seek to regain control by disregarding formal nomination procedures. Some parties may even lack formal procedures and nominations may be carried out in an ad-hoc manner. In other words, the level of institutionalization of nomination rules – and thus potentially the risk of violence – may vary. Figure 3 shows variation in the level of institutionalization of rules for selecting parliamentary candidates among the parties in our sample.[53]

Figure 3 shows that the experts indicate that only 27% of the parties in our sample have clearly stated rules that are followed by all actors involved in the process. Most of the parties (51%) have clear rules, but these rules are known to be disregarded. This conspicuous disregard for formal rules creates unpredictability in the nomination process and may, as in the cases of Kenya and Zambia, be conducive to nomination violence (see Wanyama and Elklit and Goldring and Wahman in this issue). Finally, in 21% of our cases, the parties lack clear rules for parliamentary candidate selection.

Figure 4, which shows the level of violence during parliamentary candidate selection processes for the parties in our sample, illustrates that, according to our experts, only 28% of the parties in the sample conducted nomination processes completely free from violence and coercion. In 36% of parties in the sample, experts state that nomination violence has occurred in the form of threats. In 20% of parties, experts note few acts of physical violence. In 12% there have been many acts of physical violence and, finally, in 3% of parties in the sample violence during the nomination process has resulted in casualties according to the country experts.[54] No parties saw more than 10 casualties.

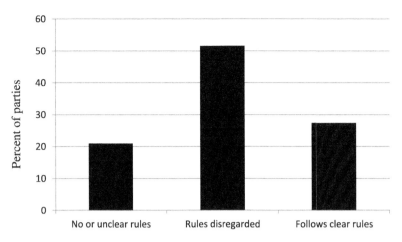

Figure 3. Institutionalization of rules for parliamentary candidate nominations across Sub-Saharan African parties.

Note: Percentage of parties displaying different degrees of institutionalization of candidate selection. "No or unclear rules" indicate that rules are informal and unclear. "Rules disregarded" indicates that there are rules, but they are disregarded either at the local or national level. "Follows clear rules" indicates that clear rules (written or unwritten) are followed. The data relate to the latest parliamentary election prior to the fall of 2016.

Figure 4 clearly shows that nomination violence is not a marginal phenomenon isolated to a handful of highly violent parties. In our sample, experts stated that it occurred in the most recent parliamentary nomination process in 72% of the parties (a total of 46 parties). However, for 18 parties (28%), the experts reported no violence. This is unsurprising. After all, certain parties are of little electoral importance, and candidates rewarded with those parties' nominations cannot be expected to gain access to any

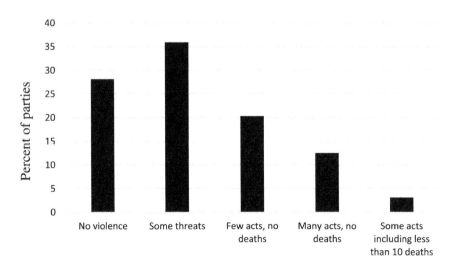

Figure 4. Violence in processes of parliamentary candidate nominations across Sub-Saharan African parties.

Note: Percent of parties that experienced various levels of violence in the most recent candidate selection process. For each party, the experts' judgements are averaged and rounded to the nearest integer. The data relate to the latest parliamentary election prior to the fall of 2016.

significant resources. To tease out variations between countries and parties, Figure 5 shows the level of nomination violence for every party in our sample.

The overview shows that in 19 out of 25 countries in our sample at least one party saw violence in relation to parliamentary nominations. The highest levels of violence registered (fatalities occurred) was seen in two parties: Uganda's NRM, and South Africa's Inkatha Freedom Party (IFP). The data also show a high degree of variation in nomination violence between countries as well as between parties within the same country. Whereas Benin, Côte d'Ivoire, Gabon, Mozambique, Namibia, and Botswana have no nomination violence recorded for any of their parties, nomination violence is a serious problem for most parties in countries like Nigeria, Chad, and South Africa according to the country experts.

Notably, nomination violence is not restricted to authoritarian systems. Parties in more democratic South Africa and Kenya have levels of violence equal to those in significantly more authoritarian Uganda and Zimbabwe. Furthermore, although majoritarian electoral systems have been argued to provoke higher levels of general election violence[55] and single-member districts could also be expected to increase the risk of nomination violence, one of the relatively few PR systems on the continent – South Africa – still see relatively high levels of nomination violence across several parties according to the experts.

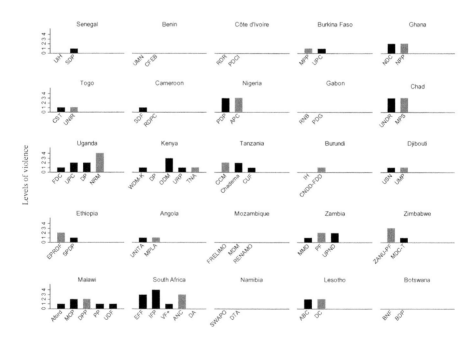

Figure 5. Violence in processes of parliamentary candidate nominations displayed by party.

Note: Levels of violence for African parties as judged by experts (the average of expert judgements for each party is taken and rounded to the nearest integer). Grey bars indicate election winners. On the y-axis, 0 indicates "There were no acts of physical violence and no threats"; 1 "There were no acts of physical violence but some threats"; 2 "There were only a few acts of physical violence. There were no deaths, but a few were injured"; 3 "There were many acts of physical violence including injuries and threats but no deaths"; 4 "There were some acts of physical violence. They resulted in less than 10 people dead"; 5 "There were many acts of physical violence. They resulted in more than 10 people dead"; 6: "There were many acts of physical violence. They resulted in more than 100 people dead". Scores relate to the latest parliamentary election prior to the fall of 2016.

In addition, the data show the need to distinguish between nomination violence and general election violence. There seems to be a general correlation between the level of violence in nominations and violence in elections overall. For instance, Nigeria – a country with fatal nomination violence in both major parties – is also known for high levels of general election violence.[56] Similarly, Namibia and Botswana, two cases free of nomination violence, according to our experts, have also had low levels of general election violence.[57] However, there is far from a one-to-one relationship between nomination and general election violence. For instance, Côte d'Ivoire, a country with devastating levels of election violence during interparty competition, has surprisingly low levels of nomination violence.[58]

In three cases, i.e. Kenya, Uganda, and Zimbabwe, the party with the highest level of nomination violence scores two categories higher than any other party in the system. In Uganda and Zimbabwe, the violence-stricken parties, NRM and ZANU-PF, are nationally dominant parties. In Kenya, the party that experiences most violence, ODM, is an opposition party in a political system with high levels of competition at the national level. However, ODM is arguably more regionally dominant than any other party in the Kenyan party system.[59] Although it is not always the case that incumbent parties have the highest level of nomination violence, Figure 6 generally suggests that incumbents – particularly dominant incumbents – tend to have higher levels of violence than their opposition (see also Reeder and Seeberg in this issue).[60] It is, however, important to acknowledge that the difference in average levels of nomination violence across the three groups (dominant incumbent, incumbent, and opposition) is rather small.

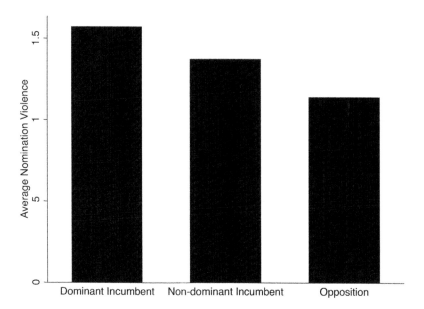

Figure 6. Average levels of nomination violence by party-type.

Note: The average level of violence is taken across the five categories where 0 indicates "There were no acts of physical violence and no threats" and 5 indicates "There were many acts of physical violence. They resulted in more than 10 people dead". Dominant incumbents have won three consecutive national elections and won an outright majority in parliament.

Conclusion

This article has attempted to set the stage for a new research agenda on candidate selection, intra-party democracy, and violence. Intra-party violence has received scant attention. However, intra-party violence during processes of candidate selection is not only a particular form of election violence that threatens to compromise the overall quality of the national election. It also jeopardizes the quality of democracy within the party institutions that are expected to help consolidate democracy in the longer term. Thus, we stress that nomination violence is likely to have serious consequences beyond the nomination period. It threatens to derail processes of democratization and undermine the consolidation of democracy.

Our expert survey shows that violence during candidate nominations is common in African parties and that it varies across parties even within the same party system. However, we know remarkably little about the roots of this violence. If levels of nomination violence differ between parties within the same party system, they cannot be fully accounted for by the common explanatory factors used to explain election violence (including conflict history and electoral system), which mostly vary on the national level. Our expert survey data, along with the contributions to this special issue, thus indicates that the causes of nomination violence are not identical to those of general election violence. This special issue emphasizes the role of party dominance and competitiveness and the institutionalization and inclusiveness of selection procedures for violence during nomination periods. Weak party institutionalization, lack of intra-party democracy, and local party dominance is characteristic for political competition in much of Africa according to the contributions. As indicated by our survey, the institutionalization and inclusiveness of selection procedures vary across African parties and their effect on nomination violence could fruitfully be analysed further.

However, these factors are by no means unique to the African continent. Scholars focusing on new democracies in other world regions have often described party politics in a very similar manner.[61] Further research outside the African continent would greatly enhance our theoretical and empirical understanding of nomination violence as a global problem impeding the process of democratic consolidation.

The individual articles in this special issue leverage a wealth of individual country experiences from around Africa and use a number of empirical strategies to add much needed nuance to our understanding of the consequences and effects of nomination violence. Our hope is that the findings will contribute to our theoretical and empirical understanding of nomination violence and that they will prove useful to democracy promoters actively engaged in increasing the level of intra-party democracy in new democracies.

Notes

1. Rakner and van de Walle, "Opposition Weakness in Africa"; Lynch and Crawford, "Democratization in Africa 1990–2010"; Cheeseman, *Democracy in Africa.*
2. Levitsky and Way, *Competitive Authoritarianism.*
3. Bhasin and Gandhi, "Timing and Targeting of State Repression in Authoritarian Elections."
4. Bogaards and Elischer, "Democratization and Competitive Authoritarianism."
5. E.g. Hyden and Leys, "Elections and Politics in Single-Party Systems"; Chazan, "African Voters at the Polls."

6. See the empirical analysis of the effect of low inter-party competition in Reeder and Seeberg in this issue.
7. Gallagher and Marsh, *Candidate Selection in Comparative Perspective.*
8. According to our data, presented later in this article, 21 out of the 25 countries in our sample had at least one party that experienced violence in the nomination process prior to the latest election.
9. Basedau, "Ethnicity and Party Preference in Africa"; Elischer, *Political Parties in Africa*; Wahman, "Nationalized Incumbents and Regional Challengers."
10. Dunning, "Fighting and Voting"; Goldsmith, "Electoral Violence in Africa Revisited."
11. Birch, *Electoral Malpractice*; van Ham and Lindberg, "From Sticks to Carrots."
12. Norris, *Why Elections Fail.*
13. Bratton, "Vote Buying and Violence."
14. Electoral authoritarian regimes, according to the definition of Schedler (*The Politics of Uncertainty*, 2) are regimes that formally establish the institutions of liberal democracy, but subvert them in practice by systematic manipulation
15. Lindberg, "What Accountability Pressures do MPs in Africa Face"; Ichino and Nathan, "Primaries on Demand?"
16. We acknowledge that non-violent forms of manipulation also distort nomination processes in both democracies and autocracies – and that the trade-off between violent and non-violent forms of manipulation is an interesting object of study (see for instance van Ham and Lindberg "From Sticks to Carrots") – but we restrict the attention of the special issue to the underexplored topic of nomination violence.
17. Höglund, Jarstad and Kovacs, "The Predicament of Elections in War-Torn Societies"; Höglund, "Electoral Violence in Conflict-Ridden Societies."
18. Höglund, Jarstad, and Kovacs, "The Predicament of Elections in War-Torn Societies"; Salehyan and Linebarger, "Elections and Social Conflict in Africa."
19. Fjelde and Höglund, "Electoral Institutions and Electoral Violence in Sub-Saharan Africa."
20. Wilkinson, *Votes and Violence*; Höglund, Jarstad, and Kovacs, "The Predicament of Elections in War-Torn Societies"; Fjelde and Höglund, "Electoral Institutions and Electoral Violence in Sub-Saharan Africa"; Salehyan and Linebarger, "Elections and Social Conflict in Africa."
21. See Hazan, "Candidate Selection"; Norris, "Recruitment."
22. Norris, *Passages to Power*; Hazan and Rahat, *Democracy within Parties*; Gallagher, "Introduction."
23. Hazan and Rahat, *Democracy within Parties.*
24. We define a dominant party as a party that has won three consecutive national elections and won an outright majority in parliament (Sartori, *Parties and Party Systems*). Party systems are competitive when there is no dominant party and competitiveness increases the more equal the vote share of the winning party and the runner up.
25. Randall and Svåsand, "Party Institutionalization."
26. Höglund, "Electoral Violence in Conflict-Ridden Societies", 417.
27. PMnews Nigeria, "APC Primary."
28. Mangongera, "A New Twilight in Zimbabwe? The Military vs. Democracy."
29. Although threats ought to be part of our definition of nomination violence, it is important to acknowledge that threats are often hard to observe and that data on violence is likely to under-report on threats. For this reason some of the empirical contributions in this issue will not include threats in their measurement of violence.
30. Sisk, *Elections in Fragile States.*
31. Ranney, "Candidate Selection", 75.
32. Gallagher, "Introduction"; Hazan and Rahat, *Democracy within Parties.*
33. Ranney, "Candidate Selection", 103.
34. Reilly and Reynolds, *Electoral Systems and Conflict in Divided Societies*; Fjelde and Höglund, "Electoral Institutions and Electoral Violence."
35. Rahat and Hazan, "Candidate Selection Methods", 298.
36. Rahat and Hazan, "Candidate Selection Methods", 298–309; see also Gallagher, "Introduction"; Ashiagbor, *Political Parties and Democracy.*
37. Ashiagbor, *Political Parties and Democracy*, 8.
38. Hazan, "Candidate Selection", 108.
39. See (e.g.) Siavelis and Morgenstern, *Pathways to Power.*

40. Teorell and Hadenius, "Pathways."
41. Senegal, Benin, Cote d'Ivoire, Burkina Faso, Ghana, Togo, Cameroon, Nigeria, Gabon, Chad, Uganda, Kenya, Tanzania, Burundi, Djibouti, Ethiopia, Angola, Mozambique, Zambia, Zimbabwe, Malawi, South Africa, Namibia, Lesotho, and Botswana.
42. Although nomination violence can happen at every conceivable level of the political system, it has often occurred "down ballot" for positions such as Governors, MPs, mayors, and councillors. In cases where party organizations are highly personalized there will be less competition for the top ticket, but even the most personalized parties need to create coalitions of local elites to expand their reach and incorporate voters at the local level. Therefore, we focus our first effort at collecting cross-national data on parliamentary elections.
43. Nomination violence also existed in the African one-party state. However, since there are no contemporary African one-party states (Wahman, Hadenius, and Teorell, "Authoritarian Regime Types Revisited"), our inference is limited to multiparty states.
44. Flesken, "Expert Survey on Party–Citizen Linkages."
45. We chose to carry out an expert survey to make sure that the data collection was based on context-sensitive and detailed knowledge of particular cases and because of the relatively low costs compared to alternatives, such as hiring students to code the question, which would be more demanding in terms of finding the relevant information and resources. We did so well-aware that expert surveys also have some potential shortcomings, such as inconsistencies in the experts' understanding of concepts and thresholds, biases in recruitment patterns, and individual and national differences in access to and selection and weighing of evidence.
46. Coppedge et al., *V-Dem Codebook v6*.
47. Norris et al., *The Expert Survey of Perceptions*.
48. Basedau et al., "Ethnicity and Party Preference in Africa"; Elischer, *Political Parties in Africa*; Wahman, "Nationalized Incumbents and Regional Challengers."
49. Hazan and Rahat, *Democracy within Parties*, 36.
50. Bratton and van de Walle, *Democratic Experiments in Africa*.
51. For each party on each of the three questions, we have taken the average of the experts' judgements and rounded to the nearest integer.
52. We have aggregated the categories on the dimension of inclusiveness so that parties score 0 on inclusiveness if candidates are selected by the party leader or party elites. They score 1 if delegates are involved in selecting candidates either alone or along with the party leadership. They score 2 if candidates are selected by party members, supporters, and/or all voters.
53. The categories on the dimension of institutionalization have been aggregated so that parties score 0 if rules are informal and unclear, 1 if there are rules, but these are disregarded either at the local or national level, and 2 if clear rules (written or unwritten) are followed.
54. Using the timing of the survey – from July to November 2016 – as the baseline.
55. Fjelde and Höglund. "Electoral Institutions and Electoral Violence."
56. Bratton, "Vote Buying and Violence."
57. Straus and Taylor, "Democratization and Electoral Violence."
58. Strauss, "It's Sheer Horror Here."
59. Brass and Cheeseman, *Beyond Ethnic Politics*.
60. We define a dominant party as a party that has won three consecutive national elections and won an outright majority in parliament (Sartori, *Parties and Party Systems*). In cases where parties changed names, but maintained the same president we counted the new party as a continuation of the old party. We did not count parties as dominant in countries with less than three uninterrupted electoral cycles.
61. E.g. Mainwaring and Scully, *Building Democratic*; Hicken, *Building Party Systems*.

Acknowledgement

Merete Bech Seeberg and Michael Wahman are the main authors of this article, and they have contributed equally. Svend-Erik Skaaning has mainly taken part in developing the core ideas behind the article (and the special issue) and through several rounds of detailed comments. The authors would like to thank Christian Bay-Andersen, Kristian Voss Olesen, and David Ulrichsen for excellent research assistance and Yonatan Morse and Lars Svåsand for excellent comments on the paper. Merete Seeberg thanks the Electoral Integrity Project and the Kathleen Fitzpatrick Australian Laureate Fellowship, Australian Research Council, for sponsoring her research fellowship at the University of Sydney. We wish to thank the CODE research group in Aarhus, the EIP research group in Sydney, and the contributors to the special issue for helping us developing the ideas for the article and the special issue as a whole. Finally, we wish to thank participants of the EIP workshop on Contentious Elections, Conflict and Regime Transitions (Poznan, July 2016), participants of the workshop on Legitimität in jungen Demokratien (Bonn, November 2016), and the anonymous reviewers for constructive comments to the paper. The project has benefited from financial support from Innovationsfonden (4110-00002B).

Disclosure statement

No potential conflict of interest was reported by the authors.

Funding

The work was supported by Innovationsfonden [110-00002B].

Bibliography

Ashiagbor, Sefakor. *Political Parties and Democracy in Theoretical and Practical Perspectives. Selecting Candidates for Legislative Office.* Washington, D.C.: National Democratic Institute, 2008.

Basedau, Matthias, Gero Ermann, Jan Lay, and Alexander Stroh. "Ethnicity and Party Preference in sub-Saharan Africa." *Democratization* 18, no. 2 (2011): 462–489.

Bhasin, Tavishi, and Jennifer Gandhi. "Timing and Targeting of State Repression in Authoritarian Elections." *Electoral Studies* 32, no. 4 (2013): 620–631.

Birch, Sarah *Electoral Malpractice.* Oxford: Oxford University Press, 2011.

Bogaards, Matthijs, and Sebastian Elischer. "Democratization and Competitive Authoritarianism in Africa Revisited." *Zeitschrift für Vergleichende Politikwissenschaft* 10, no. 6 (2016): 5–18.

Brass, Jennifer, and Nic Cheeseman. "Beyond Ethnic Politics: The Limits of Bloc-Voting in Kenya." *Unpublished Manuscript*, 2013.

Bratton, Michael. "Vote Buying and Violence in Nigerian Election Campaigns." *Electoral Studies* 27, no. 4 (2008): 621–632.

Bratton, Michael, and Nicolas van de Walle. *Democratic Experiments in Africa: Regime Transitions in Comparative Perspective.* New York: Cambridge University Press, 1997.

Chazan, Naomi. "African Voters at the Polls: A re-Examination of the Role of Elections in African Politics." *Commonwealth and Comparative Politics* 17, no. 2 (1979): 136–158.

Cheeseman, Nic. *Democracy in Africa: Successes, Failures, and the Struggle for Political Reform.* New York: Cambridge University Press, 2015.

Conroy-Krutz, Jeffrey, and Nicholas Kerr. "Dynamics of Democratic Satisfaction in Transitional Settings: Evidence from a Panel Study in Uganda." *Political Research Quarterly* 68, no. 3 (2015): 593–606.

Coppedge, Michael, John Gerring, Staffan I. Lindberg, Svend-Erik Skaaning, Jan Teorell et al. *V-Dem Codebook v6*. Varieties of Democracy (V-Dem) Project, 2016.

Daxecker, Ursula E. "The Cost of Exposing Cheating International Election Monitoring, Fraud, and Post-Election Violence in Africa." *Journal of Peace Research* 49, no. 4 (2012): 503–516.

Dunning, Thad. "Fighting and Voting: Violent Conflict and Electoral Politics." *Journal of Conflict Resolution* 55, no. 3 (2011): 327–339.

Elischer, Sebastian. *Political Parties in Africa: Ethnicity and Party Formation*. Cambridge: Cambridge University Press, 2013.

Fjelde, Hanne, and Kristine Höglund. "Electoral Institutions and Electoral Violence in Sub-Saharan Africa." *British Journal of Political Science* 46, no. 2 (2016): 297–320.

Flesken, Anaïd. 2017. *Expert Survey on Party–Citizen Linkages. Interim Report on the Results*. Bristol: University of Bristol.

Gallagher, Michael. "Introduction." In *Candidate Selection in Comparative Perspective: The Secret Garden of Politics*, edited by Michael Gallagher and Michael Marsh, 1–19. London: Sage, 1988.

Gallagher, Michael, and Michael Marsh, eds. *Candidate Selection in Comparative Perspective: The Secret Garden of Politics*. London: Sage, 1988.

Giollabhuí, Shane Mac. "How Things Fall Apart: Candidate Selection and the Cohesion of Dominant Parties in South Africa and Namibia." *Party Politics* 52, no. 4 (2013): 577–600.

Goldsmith, Arthur A. "Elections and Civil Violence in New Multiparty Regimes: Evidence From Africa." *Journal of Peace Research* 52, no. 5 (2015): 607–621.

Goldsmith, Arthur A. "Electoral Violence in Africa Revisited." *Terrorism and Political Violence* 27, no. 5 (2015): 818–837.

Hadenius, Axel, and Jan Teorell. "Pathways from Authoritarianism." *Journal of Democracy* 18, no. 1 (2007): 143–157.

Hafner-Burton, Emilie M., Susan D. Hyde, and Ryan S. Jablonski. "When Do Governments Resort to Election Violence?" *British Journal of Political Science* 44, no. 1 (2014): 149–179.

Hazan, Reuven Y. "Candidate Selection." In *Comparing Democracies 2: Elections and Voting in Global Perspective*, edited by Lawrence LeDuc, Richard G. Niemi, and Pippa Norris, 108–126. London: Sage, 2002.

Hazan, Reuven Y., and Gideon Rahat. *Democracy within Parties: Candidate Selection Methods and Their Political Consequences*. Oxford, New York: Oxford University Press, 2010.

Hicken, Allen. *Building Party Systems in Developing Democracies*. Cambridge: Cambridge University Press, 2009.

Höglund, Kristine. "Electoral Violence in Conflict-Ridden Societies: Concepts, Causes, and Consequences." *Terrorism and Political Violence* 21, no. 3 (2009): 412–427.

Höglund, Kristine, Anna K. Jarstad, and Mimmi Söderberg Kovacs. "The Predicament of Elections in War-Torn Societies." *Democratization* 16, no. 3 (2009): 530–557.

Ichino, Nahomi, and Noah Nathan. "Primaries on Demand? Intra-Party Politics and Nominations in Ghana." *British Journal of Political Science* 42, no. 4 (2012): 769–791.

Lebas, Adrienne. *From Protests to Parties: Party-Building and Democratization in Africa*. Oxford: Oxford University Press, 2011.

Levitsky, Steven, and Lucan Way. *Competitive Authoritarianism: Hybrid Regimes After the Cold War*. New York: Cambridge University Press, 2010.

Lindberg, Staffan. "What Accountability Pressures Do MPs in Africa Face and How Do They Respond? Evidence From Ghana" *The Journal of Modern African Studies* 48, no. 1 (2010): 117–142.

Lynch, Gabrielle, and Gordon Crawford. "Democratization in Africa 1990–2010: An Assessment." *Democratization* 18, no. 2 (2011): 275–310.

Mainwaring, Scott, and Timothy Scully, eds. *Building Democratic Institutions: Party Systems in Latin America*. Notre Dame: Notre Dame University Press, 1995.

Mangongera, Charles. "A New Twilight in Zimbabwe? The Military vs. Democracy." *Journal of Democracy* 25, no. 2 (2014): 67–76.

Mansfield, Edward, and Jack Snyder. *Electing to Fight: Why Emerging Democracies Go to War*. Cambridge: MIT Press, 2005.

Morse, Yonatan. "From Single-Party to Electoral Authoritarian Regimes: The Institutional Origins of Competitiveness in Post-Cold War Africa." *Comparative Politics* 48, no. 1 (2015): 126–151.

Norris, Pippa. Ferran Martínez i Coma, Alessandro Nai, and Max Groemping. *The Expert Survey of Perceptions of Electoral Integrity*, 2016, *PEI_4.0*. www.electoralintegrityproject.com.

Norris, Pippa, ed. *Passages to Power: Legislative Recruitment in Advanced Democracies*. New York: Cambridge University Press, 1997.

Norris, Pippa. "Recruitment." In *Handbook of Party Politics*, edited by Richard S. Katz and William J. Crotty, 89–108. London: SAGE Publications, 2006.

Norris, Pippa. *Why Elections Fail*. New York: Cambridge University Press, 2015.

Norris, Pippa, Richard W. Frank, and Ferran Martínez i Coma, eds. *Contentious Elections. From Ballots to Barricades*. New York: Routledge, 2015.

PMnewsnigeria. *APC Primary Ends in Violence*. 05/27/2017. https://www.pmnewsnigeria.com/2017/05/27/apc-primary-ends-violence/.

Rahat, Gideon, and Reuven Y. Hazan. "Candidate Selection Methods: An Analytical Framework." *Party Politics* 7, no. 3 (2001): 297–322.

Rakner, Lise, and Nic van de Walle. "Opposition Weakness in Africa." *Journal of Democracy* 20, no. 3 (2009): 108–121.

Randall, Vicky, and Lars Svåsand. "Party Institutionalization in New Democracies." *Party Politics*, 8, no. 1 (2002): 5–29.

Ranney, Austin. 1981. "Candidate Selection." In *Democracy at the Polls*, edited by David Butler, Howard R. Penniman, and Austin Ranney, 75–106. Washington,DC: American Enterprise Institute.

Reilly, Ben, and Andrew Reynolds. *Electoral Systems and Conflict in Divided Societies*. Papers on International Conflict Resolution No. 2. Washington, DC: National Academy Press, 1999.

Riedl, Rachel. *Authoritarian Origins of Democratic Party Systems in Africa*. New York: Cambridge University Press, 2014.

Salehyan, Idean, and Christopher Linebarger. "Elections and Social Conflict in Africa, 1990–2009." *Studies in Comparative International Development* 50, no. 1 (2015): 23–49.

Sartori, Gionvanni. *Parties and Party Systems: A Framework for Analysis*. Colchester: ECPR Press, 2005.

Schedler, Andreas. 2013. *The Politics of Uncertainty: Sustaining and Subverting Electoral Authoritarianism*. Oxford: Oxford University Press.

Siavelis, Peter, and Scott Morgenstern, eds. *Pathways to Power: Political Recruitment and Candidate Selection in Latin America*. University Park: The Pennsylvania State University Press, 2008.

Sisk, Timothy. "Elections in Fragile States: Between Voice and Violence." Prepared for The international studies association annual meeting, San Francisco, March 24–28, 2008.

Straus, Scott. "'It's Sheer Horror Here': Patterns of Violence during the First Four Months of Côte d'Ivoire's Post-Election Crisis." *African Affairs* 110, no. 440 (2011): 481–489.

Straus, Scott, and Charles Taylor. 2012. "Democratization and Electoral Violence in SSA, 1990–2008." In *Voting in Fear*, edited by Dorina Bekoe, 15–38. Washington,D.C.: United States Institute of Peace Press.

Van Eerd, Jonathan. *The Quality of Democracy in Africa*. Cham: Palgrave, 2017.

Van Ham, Carolien, and Staffan Lindberg. "From Sticks to Carrots: Electoral Manipulation in Africa, 1986–2012." *Government and Opposition* 50, no. 3 (2015): 521–548.

von Borzyskowski, Inken. "A Double-Edged Sword: International Influence on Election Violence." *Unpublished Dissertation*, University of Wisconsin, 2014.

Wahman, Michael. "Nationalized Incumbents and Regional Challengers: Opposition- and Incumbent-Party Nationalization in Africa." *Party Politics* 23, no. 3 (2017): 309–322.

Wahman, Michael, Jan Teorell, and Axel Hadenius. "Authoritarian Regime Types Revisited: Updated Data in Comparative Perspective." *Contemporary Politics* 19, no. 1 (2013): 19–34.

Wilkinson, Steven I. *Votes and Violence: Electoral Competition and Ethnic Riots in India*. New York: Cambridge University Press, 2006.

Zambiareports.com. *Riots Among Ruling Party Factions Hit Lusaka*. 12/2014/02. https://zambiareports.com/2014/12/02/riots-among-ruling-party-factions-hit-lusaka/.

Battleground: candidate selection and violence in Africa's dominant political parties

Shane Mac Giollabhui

ABSTRACT

This article develops a theory – rooted in the experience of the African National Congress in South Africa – to explain how, and why, a dominant political party is less likely to conduct orderly elections to select its political leadership. First, I demonstrate that canny party leaders – operating in the space between a divided society and a weak state – make an ideological turn to a "congress-like" political party, which is clever (in the short term) because it provides party leaders with an in-built electoral majority. It is, however, also a dangerous manoeuvre because it essentially endogenizes social competition for state resources inside the dominant party. This displacement of social competition away from the public sphere towards the partisan organization increases the likelihood of disorderly competition for party candidacies. Second, I demonstrate how this competition need not necessarily become the basis of violent competition inside the dominant party. The party leadership can use intra-party elections to stabilize competition, but only if the party invests in an organization that applies impartially the rules that govern the election.

Introduction

This article addresses two questions. First, why do some political parties conduct orderly elections to select political candidates, while in other parties, these selection contests descend into violent disorder?[1] Second, if we can explain why some selection contests become more than a figurative battle, can we make a prediction about why some political parties are more vulnerable to an outbreak of violence inside their ranks? I examine these questions in one type of party: the "dominant party" that selects candidates "democratically".[2] It is an important category because it is both populous and, as the introduction to this special issue underlines, populated by some of the most violent cases in this study. It is also interesting because it seems so implausible, unsettling even, that a party that governs itself democratically might be disproportionately violent. It follows that an unstable political party – especially an unstable *dominant* party – can undermine democratic stability.[3]

It is surprising but nonetheless true that the existing literature on African political parties does not provide a theoretical or empirical road map to study intra-party relationships. There is a preponderance of research on various aspects of party *systems*, including their classification,[4] sources of fragmentation,[5] level of institutionalization[6] and nationalization,[7] and social basis[8] – but there is very little work on the type of processes at work inside party *organizations*. This imbalance is not coincidental: it is notoriously difficult to conduct research on the content of African political parties, rather than the metadata that describes African party systems (effective number of seats, volatility of support, manifesto policy position, legal status, and so on).

There is also a fundamental reluctance to study party organization in Africa, which can be traced to a stubborn tendency to dismiss African political parties as *sui generis*.[9] If researchers do look inside individual cases, the emphasis is often on ethnicity rather than organization.[10] The prevailing narrative, then, raises a standard lament that African political parties, as a rule, are little more than "political cabals or clubs", dominated by the charismatic personalities of their leaders.[11] But if this orthodox view of African parties is accurate, how can we explain such intense and at times violent competition between rival candidates for selection as a party candidate? If the competition involves a stable cast of protagonists, unfolds on a party stage, and becomes in timing and conduct an almost ritualistic part of the election cycle, does it not follow that it is organized?

I contend that canny party leaders – operating in the space between a divided society and a weak state – make an ideological turn to a "congress-like" political party, which provides an institutional mechanism to govern authoritatively.[12] This strategic turn is clever in the short term because it essentially endogenizes social tensions inside its ranks, which provides party leaders with an in-built electoral majority, but it is also dangerous because it displaces social competition for state resources away from the *public* sphere to the *partisan* organization. This competition, in turn, can degenerate into conflict for privileged access to state resources, which places an onus on party leaders to design a system that can regulate factional conflict in an orderly manner.[13] I contend that intra-party elections can provide the basis for orderly competition, but *only if* there is an impartial party agency to regulate this electoral competition inside the party's ranks.

The article's road map is as follows. First, I describe how the dominant party became a party "machine" that *endogenizes* conflict between its constituent formations, who compete to secure privileged access to state patronage. Second, I develop an explanatory typology that outlines how intra-party elections incentivize orderly competition for candidacies, but *only if* the party invests in a mechanism to guarantee these elections are conducted lawfully. Third, I apply this theory to analyse how the African National Congress (South Africa) has managed to conduct orderly competition inside its ranks. Fourth, I draw lessons from the case that speak directly to the community of policy-makers who fund political parties. Fifth, I conclude with some general statements about the relationship between party organization and democratization.

The turn to party in postcolonial Africa

Independence is a critical juncture in the history of modern African states. It is a moment of pride for "new" states, but also a moment of vulnerability for new state leaders, who – in the face of popular and competing pressure to redistribute wealth –

needed to devise a strategy to govern authoritatively in a weak state. State leaders have the option to choose one of two roads at this juncture: the institutional route (leaders invest in a national organization to broadcast power) or the personal route (leaders dismantle institutions and rule patrimonially).[14] The institutional road is the harder and less travelled road because it takes a certain type of political acumen to appreciate that while institutions constrain, institutions also empower. In this section, I describe how some leaders turned to the political party as the ideological and institutional solution to the dilemma of how to govern authoritatively in a weak state. These leaders created *dominant* political parties, which stabilized (fragile) regimes by acting as a site to regulate social competition for (scarce) public resources.

The genetic origin of the dominant party can be traced to the weakness of the archetypal state in Africa, which has rarely, if ever, exercised a monopoly over the legitimate use of violence inside its territorial boundaries. The weakness of the state's central authority means that while a state may have full juridical sovereignty, its empirical content is low.[15] In order to govern such vast (and "uncaptured") expanses of territory, colonial administrators empowered "traditional" leaders to rule indirectly, while encouraging private corporate enterprises to invest in an infrastructure – located, primarily, in new capital cities, presided over by a bureaucratic elite – to coordinate the extraction, transportation, and export of mineral and agricultural commodities.[16] This policy produced a peculiarly dissonant sociological outcome. It established ethnicity – rather than occupation or religion – as the single most important dimension of a person's political identity, but by making traditional leaders complicit in the colonial project, it simultaneously demolished their legitimacy.

This elevation of ethnicity as the primary social cleavage is a defining feature of the colonial legacy, which produced – according to Joel Migdal – a strong society that exists alongside a weak state.[17] The "strong society, weak state" formula has an axiomatic status in the study of African politics, but how does it help us theorize the dominant party in African politics? The short answer is that every party leader in Africa who inherited a weak state occupied a position of extreme "vulnerability", which left the leadership of these new governments with a decision about how to manage their exposure to the sudden wave of popular pressure.[18] This pressure was manifested in two ways. The new government of each state was not just incapacitated by the "extreme weakness" of the state,[19] which made it vulnerable to the sudden opening of a "floodgate of claimants", who pressed hard to secure privileged access to the resources of the state,[20] but these governments also had to think about how the transfer of power had produced a "frenzied attempt, through political organization, to maximize the position of one's primordial [sic] group in the new and uncertain civil order".[21]

This pressure on the government to deal with economic inequality and social fragmentation produced a "strain" on the fledgling state which, according to a White Paper of Nkrumah's government in Ghana, was equivalent to the strain on a "developed country in wartime".[22] The moment of independence, then, provoked a crisis, which demanded a response from party and state leaders: how to deal with the "staggering problems of nation-building and modernization".[23] It provoked what historical institutionalists call a critical juncture, because it forced African leaders to make a choice about how to govern their divided territories. It provoked, in particular, a dilemma about whether to turn to the political party. It made sense because the national movement was "the most visible, immediately available" and perhaps the only national organization that could tackle the twin problems of economic modernization and national integration.[24] But it was also a risky move because the empowerment of the party organizations would ultimately constrain the autonomy of party leaders.[25]

In many, perhaps most, African cases, the leadership eschewed the institutional option and chose, instead, to dismantle the political party and all other institutionalized avenues of civil and political opposition.[26] In some cases, however, political leaders made a deliberate *ideological* turn to the political party as an instrument that could provide "an integrative and stabilizing structure" and "an organizational means for conflict resolution".[27] The ideologues of the dominant party become the autocrats of the one-party state, so we should treat their motivations with scepticism – but, if we look at the ideology of the one-party state as a political theory alone, we can see how it is designed explicitly to manage conflict. Sékou Touré writes forcefully (and in the Marxian terminology of the day) about how the "internal contradictions of our societies" can only be resolved if all parties unite into a "single anti-colonialist front". It might have been self-serving, but – as an abstract construct – it was at least plausible that in a divided society, the political party was a type of necessary evil because, in its absence, political order becomes unlikely in "nations [that] rest on such shaky foundations and are confronted by such urgent and monumental task of integration and development".[28]

The purpose of this article is not to disinter the reputations of dead ideologues, but if we accept that many (vulnerable) leaders acted in good faith out of a sense of institutional necessity and ideological conviction, it follows that the turn to party was not an elaborate feint, but rather a genuine attempt to activate the political party to perform two important functions: first, brokering the state's relationship with its citizens; and, second, providing a site to accommodate competing social formations. The transformation of the nationalist movement into a political party that *endogenized* competition across social cleavages – rather than acting as an outcrop of a single social formation – is an important moment in the history of African political parties. It establishes the template of a viable institutional mechanism – a prototype, in fact, of the modern dominant party – that political leaders have turned to consistently to strengthen their (weak) grip on power, but it also displaced social competition from the public sphere to the private organization of the party, which in turn has made the dominant party uniquely vulnerable to disorder inside its ranks.

The dominant party, then, becomes a space inhabited by a plurality of social categories, who competed – in the party's earliest days as a nationalist movement – for control of the movement's ideological direction. This benign character, however, undergoes a dramatic change when the movement enters office as a party of government. First, the "chief" centralizes power in the office of the executive, which becomes "the dominant institution in the one-party state".[29] Second, this power is used to inflate and politicize the public sector, which opens up a source of patronage to reward allies and co-opt rival elites.[30] Third, the ideologues of the one-party state write a script that imbues the dominant party with a moral character, which simultaneously invalidates the legitimacy of an opposition. Fourth, the president copper-fastens this *de facto* dominance by re-writing the institutional rules to either, in some cases, create *de jure* one-party states (Tanzania, 1965; Zambia, 1972; Kenya, 1982) or simply make opposition politically unviable (Côte d'Ivoire, 1960; Kenya 1969, Senegal 1966).[31] Finally, and critically, the state leadership transforms the dominant party into a "machine" to regulate the distribution of state resources to loyal constituencies, which had a sound short-term logic, but it raised considerably the stakes of political competition inside the dominant party.[32]

The construction of the dominant party provided an institutional and ideological solution to the regulatory problem of how to govern authoritatively in a weak state. It was not, however, the first step on the road to democracy, even if the dominant party had some democratic characteristics. There is undeniably an ideological purity in the origin of the dominant party, but when the dominant party became fused to state structures it transformed into a machine that regulated popular access to public resources, which destroyed its moral legitimacy and (in many, if not all cases) had a ruinous effect on the provision of public goods. If this reading of the dominant party as an institutional safety valve is correct, it reverses our understanding of the relationship between candidate selection and violence in Africa's dominant party systems. It suggests that dominant parties are not more prone to disorderly competition, but rather that fierce – and, indeed, on occasion violent – competition for candidacies is *endogenous* to the dominant party in Africa.

Candidate selection and violence in Africa's dominant political parties

The question, then, more precisely is not just about how a political party conducts an orderly contest to select public representatives; the question, in a dominant political party, becomes: how does a party design a system that allows a dominant party to maintain its cohesion, but not descend into a violent competition for state resources?[33] The literature on party "institutionalization" is a useful point of departure, which sets out a wide range of factors – an autonomous leadership, a coherent infrastructure, a set of values, roots in society – that help describe the process that leads to a party's acquisition of value and stability. This literature provides useful lines of inquiry for this study, but its multi-dimensional approach is also its great weakness because the literature, according to Vicky Randall and Lars Svåsand, "fail[s] to identify clearly what the relationship is between the different dimensions and institutionalization. Are they causes or prerequisites; are they intrinsic characteristics; or are they indicators or consequences?"[34]

If there is any way through this pea soup of a literature, it lies unquestionably in a reductive approach. I believe the elemental issue is whether the party's leader(ship) is willing to invest in a party organization. It seems obvious that this investment is *necessary*, but it is also deeply problematic because it involves a sharp reduction in the personal power of the leader(ship). And why would any leadership "accept that partial *diminutio capitis*, that reduction in personal power", even if it is, as Angelo Panebianco made clear, "indispensable to organizational institutionalization?"[35] The sharpest point of this diminution involves investing in a system to select the party leadership that is *beyond* the control of the leadership. The development of this kind of "succession" system, according to Samuel Huntington, is a "major turning point" in the consolidation of a party because it helps resolve the "inherent conflict between personal leadership and party institutionalization".[36]

If a leader makes this investment in a mechanism to regulate competition between ambitious partisans for coveted posts, a (personal) political vehicle becomes an (organized) political party.[37] This investment in organization is an *elemental* property of a political party, but its application is variable. The ideal leadership makes a credible commitment to establish a *neutral* agency, which acts as a referee to interpret and enforce the party's "rule of law" in internal competitions to select the party leadership. If there is no formal agency, the leadership makes an informal or tacit commitment to remain above the fray, as it were, in the process of candidate selection. We can hypothesize that, ceteris paribus, if the national leadership – or a faction of the national leadership – intervenes "unlawfully" in a local contest to select candidates, this interference will provide local contestants with a legitimate grievance that might, in turn, form the moral justification to turn to violence.

If a party leadership does empower the party organization to (re)produce the party leadership, it can – once this neutral agency is in position – design a wide variety of different types of electoral mechanisms to select candidates (see Seeberg et al. (2018) in the introduction).[38] It follows that different types of selection system can produce, or discourage, disorderly competition between candidates. I am interested in one sub-type of system: the party that uses a democratic method to select candidates. I am interested, in particular, in one type of political party: the dominant party that competes in a proportional electoral system. This category includes the ANC in South Africa, which is the centrepiece of this article's later empirical analysis. It is a substantially interesting case because Closed-List PR, unlike Single-Member Plurality systems, is "the only family of [electoral] systems in which there is no role for the electoral rules in allocating seats to candidates".[39] Closed-List PR, in other words, gives the party leadership total control over the design of its internal selection processes.

The empirical examination of this type of system invites a prior question: why would the party leadership make the counter-intuitive decision to *democratize* the process of selection, when it could legitimately empower a much smaller – and, presumably, more biddable – selectorate to nominate public representatives? The literature on elections in authoritarian regimes suggests a clear resolution to the apparent paradox of party primaries: leaders use elections as a device to stabilize a ruling coalition (the dominant party). The canny autocrat uses elections to acquire valuable information about opponents, signal strength to rivals, distribute patronage efficiently, and monitor supporters at the local level.[40] The effect, according to Barbara Geddes, is a striking difference in the durability of autocracies that use elections compared to regimes that do not.[41] It follows, too, that party leaders can use party primaries in precisely the same way – which raises a reasonable suspicion that party leaders use party primaries as a system of "competitive clientelism" to create a stable mechanism to regulate access to state patronage, which redistributes patronage efficiently (to loyal supporters), but also provides a way to keep these local brokers in check.[42]

If party leaders enfranchise the party membership to stabilize the regime, rather than out of any high-minded normative commitment to democracy inside the party, how might the leadership design this system? Do party leaders open up *all* executive offices to selection from below? Is the party president popularly elected, or is the competition restricted to lesser party offices? And who, precisely, is enfranchised to select this leadership? Does the "selectorate" include all citizens (the open primary), or all members (the closed primary), or just a sub-set of members and party officials? We can speculate that different types of "selection systems" lead to varying levels of disorder – up to and including violent disorder – inside a political party? We can hypothesize that a more inclusive system is, all other things being equal, more likely to stabilize competition – partly because it legitimizes the winner of the contest, but also because it provides the loser with a reliable return route to power at the next (s)election contest. If the leadership shuts down this avenue, I expect that it will raise significantly the likelihood of violence in the local contest – not simply because it closes the "return route" that encourages a losing candidate to accept defeat,[43] but also because it damages the local party candidate's trust that the party centre can act credibly as a neutral agent to arbitrate fairly.

It is possible, now, to use the literature on party institutionalization to generate a parsimonious framework that prioritizes two explanatory factors: party organization (neutral or biased) and candidate selection systems (inclusive or exclusive) – that might help explain why some parties conduct orderly competition for political candidacies, while competitions in other parties descend into violent disorder. Figure 1 presents a two-by-two table, which illustrates the variables' interactive relationship, which is the core theoretical statement in this article. I contend that inclusive procedures will encourage orderly competition (and maintain party cohesion), but *only if* there is a neutral party agency to regulate this competition (Type 1). If, conversely, the party uses an inclusive procedure to select its leadership, but does not have a neutral party agency to referee the contest, we are more likely to see a disorderly selection contest, although this disorder is unlikely to threaten the cohesion of the party (Type 2). The third and fourth categories characterize the counter-factual: if a dominant party centralizes control over candidate selection, but still nonetheless selects these candidates according to the party's rules, it will destabilize the party, but not necessarily produce disorderly competition (Type 3). A centralized party that does not follow its own rule book, on the other hand, is more likely than any other category of party to collapse in disarray (Type 4).

If this typology provides a valid theoretical account of how a political party can encourage orderly competition for political candidacies, it ought to shed light on the dynamics of social competition inside Africa's dominant political parties. I apply this framework to analyse an important case of party dominance: the ANC in South Africa. The case study is based on interviews with a wide range of figures inside the ANC during the course of successive fieldtrips, which were conducted in 2005/06,

		Candidate Selection System	
		Inclusive	Exclusive
Party Organization	Neutral	Type 1: Cohesive/ Orderly	Type 3: Incohesive/ Orderly
	Partisan	Type 2: Cohesive/ Disorderly	Type 4: Incohesive/ Disorderly

Figure 1. Explanatory typology of candidate selection procedures and impact on party cohesion and order.

2011 and 2013. I interviewed approximately 75 members of the party, some on several occasions over time, including members of the party's National Executive Committee (NEC), National Working Committee, office-bearers in the senior leadership, members of parliament, and senior cabinet ministers. I selected informants from across the party's constituent components (geographic and sectoral) who could provide a broad range of opinions about the "state of the party". I provided each informant with a guarantee of anonymity, but made clear that the material would be used for the production of public research.

South Africa has a proportional electoral system, Closed-List PR, which is used every five years to elect the 400 members of the state's lower house of parliament (the National Assembly). Voters select a single political party on the ballot sheet, which determines each party's share of the vote. There are two tiers of allocation to translate votes into seats: a set of nine "provincial" districts (in proportion to the area's population) and a national district (with 200 members), which compensates for any disproportionality in the provincial allocations. The allocation in both tiers is conducted according to the Droop formula. There is, effectively, no disproportionality in the South African system: the "cost" of a seat in the most recent national general election (2014) was just over 30,000 votes (out of almost eighteen and a half million valid votes). This extreme level of proportionality places South Africa among the most permissive electoral systems in the world.[44]

This electoral system establishes two important parameters in the application (and extension) of the explanatory typology to the case study. First, it underlines just how extraordinary it is that the ANC – operating in one of the world's most diverse societies, using one of the world's most permissive electoral systems – is able to maintain such a broad coalition of support inside its ranks. There are few, if any, structural obstacles to the formation of new parties; the electoral system's "barrier to entry" is, effectively, non-existent, which permits the leadership of a breakaway faction inside the ANC to consider more readily the option to "exit" the party. In other systems with a higher barrier to entry, the logic of intra-party competition will change accordingly. Second, the electoral system does not present the ANC with a legally binding method to select candidates; the ANC, as it happens, selects candidates to mirror the "locus" electoral systems configuration – the nine provinces nominate nine lists, while the national executive signs off on a national list – but Closed-List PR gives the ANC total flexibility to enfranchise as many, or as few, "electors" as it wishes to select the party's leadership.

In spite of the permissiveness of the electoral system, and diversity of its society, the ANC has maintained its broad social coalition since 1994. The party governs South Africa as the principal member of the Tripartite Alliance, which includes the Congress of South Africa Trade Unions and the South African Communist Party. This broad sectional coalition of left-wing constituencies is the mainstay of the ANC's electoral dominance – the continued loyalty of the Alliance partners is the main barometer of ANC cohesion – but the ANC's "congress-like" character also encompasses (historically) the full spectrum of social categories in South Africa. There are, according to one of its leaders, "socialists in the ANC, communists in the ANC, highly religious and devoted Muslims and Christians, liberals, conservatives ... everyone is in the ANC".[45] It is a party with an "exceptionally diverse" range of intellectual and ideological tendencies.[46]

The ANC, in short, is not designed to represent a single social category; it is not, in this sense, an ordinary political party. It is a party that has sought historically to *endogenize* conflict inside its ranks in order to create a space – populated by *all* major social categories – to seek national reconciliation and economic transformation. The ANC's genetic wiring as an inclusive *movement* provided a type of moral legitimacy, which was indispensable during the anti-Apartheid struggle, but this consociational character became a source of tension when the ANC entered office. The party became caught, according to Patrick Bond, in a "pincer movement" between its disenfranchised (popular) base and its (liberal) parliamentary elite, who were inclined to make the standard compromises.[47] The base, however, expanded rapidly into the party's new organization – membership of the ANC has almost tripled since independence – but while the old generation was motivated ideologically, the new generation of cadre focuses on the ANC's capacity to deliver patronage (and services). "The people who are joining the ANC today", according to one of my informants:

> are driven by one desire: to have access to power, in order for them to have access to resources and patronage. So what is dividing us now is not an ideological problem. We are just divided because every person wants to be a chairperson of a branch at all cost, in order for him then to have some access to resources and (…) the patronage system. That's what divides the ANC now.

There has been a quickening appreciation among scholars that democratic institutions, operating in the conditions of economic inequality, have "activated and expanded" social fault lines, which in turn increases the risk that these social groups compete fiercely and, at times, violently for access to state resources.[48] In a dominant party system, the ruling party – designed, as we have seen, to endogenize (and regulate) this competition, becomes the primary site of political contestation. It is hardly surprising, then, that the ANC – in spite of the tendency, bordering on a prejudice, to treat South Africa as an exceptional case[49] – has followed so closely the experience of not only Africa's "congress-like" parties in the postcolonial period, but also the experience of other liberation movements in other world regions.[50]

There is a wealth of material that documents how the party's electoral machinery has become geared primarily to pick winners in a "battle for loot".[51] Tom Lodge reports how the ANC itself concluded that competition in the party was "wholly and singularly caused by corruption … the scramble for state resources, and a tendency for local comrades to regard local structures as their own fiefdoms".[52] Alex Beresford, more recently, introduces the "gatekeeper" framework to demonstrate how the ANC has colonized the state to transform "networks of *public* authority [into] a vital facilitator of *private* capital accumulation".[53] The ANC, in the eyes of Roger Southall, has become "overwhelmed by the predatory behaviour of its elites".[54] The ANC, too, has underlined how the regime sins of incumbency" have opened up internecine competition for state resources that has pushed the party to the "cusps of paralysis".[55]

The ANC is hard-wired to produce competition inside its ranks: it is, ideologically, committed to provide an open space to accommodate competing social formation but it has become – via its electoral success – the most valuable piece of political real-estate in South Africa. When Huntington wrote that "organization is the road to political power", he might as well have been writing about the ANC.[56] There is, as a consequence, a level of "conflict and tension within the ANC", according to one MP, "that will be a constant factor. What matters for the leadership is … how does it manage these tensions?"[57] This, indeed, is the critical question: how does the ANC – a party configured to pick winners in one of the world's most unequal societies – manage to conduct the race in an orderly way?

The answer is in two parts. First, the unprescriptive nature of Closed-List PR gave the ANC the flexibility to design a candidate selection system to manage these tensions. Second, this flexibility of Closed-List PR gave the ANC space to design a system that enfranchises its million-plus membership to select branch-level delegates, who attend periodically a conference – depending on the geographic area (branch, region, and so on) – that elects the party's leadership. So, for instance, the entire national membership nominates delegates (in proportion to the size of the branch) to attend a national conference to select the party's leadership (including the president, the chief "office-bearers", and the party's NEC). These delegates use a modified version of the block-vote (a highly disproportionate electoral system) to vote for rival "slates" of candidates. The democratic nature of the elections matters because it legitimizes the winner, who is empowered to govern authoritatively. Second, the elections – or, more precisely, the prospect of future elections – provide the losers with a predictable return route to power. An informant describes the logic that works out in the mind of the unsuccessful candidate in the ANC, irrespective of whether the candidacy was branch secretary or member of the NEC.

> those who are defeated in the slate, they don't dissolve. They simply plan their comeback. We win today, but we know that already those who are defeated in the conference today, they start planning your downfall the day you win the election. It's a continuous struggle in the movement. Not in terms of refining our ideas about government, but about how to win again.[58]

In the first decade of democracy, the ANC avoided open competition for the party's national leadership, but this changed when Jacob Zuma challenged the incumbent, Thabo Mbeki, at the ANC's 52nd National Conference, which was held at the University of Limpopo (Polokwane) in December 2007.[59] Frank Chikane described it as "dramatic, rough, very hostile, and totally uncharacteristic of the ANC" – but, critically, the election at Polokwane was conducted *peacefully*. It could have spiralled out of control, but it did not.[60] Why? First, the election provided Jacob Zuma with a moral claim to the presidency, which legitimized his victory. Zuma won a convincing majority – over 60% of the delegates' votes – which, filtered through the conference's (disproportionate) electoral system, became translated into an overwhelming victory, not just for Zuma, but for his entire "slate" of candidates.

Second, President Mbeki and his supports could only have disrupted the moral basis of the victory with a rival claim that Zuma had broken to rules to win the contest. There were claims that each camp had bribed delegates to vote one way or the other, there were allegations of procedural irregularities in the accreditation of delegates, but there is a general consensus – borne out in the correlation between the breakdown of provincial nominations and the overall national result – that the delegates' vote reflected the will of the party's members. It was a critical moment, pregnant with the danger that resides in all moments of succession, but in the aftermath, President Mbeki accepted defeat graciously. A close ally, and member of the party's outgoing NEC in 2007, describes the president's behaviour:

> It [the scale of Zuma's victory] wasn't as decisive as it seems on the surface. There was enough support still for Mbeki, but the majority voted for Zuma and Mbeki was the first to accept it. There were a lot of people who complained, who said – "there was manipulation [in] the

Western Cape" – but he said, "No. The delegates have voted." And he's the first to go onto the stage to congratulate Zuma. Then those of us who were also members of the NEC went on the stage. We said, "Let's accept this election result. We can't destroy this movement."[61]

There was a lull in the ferocity of competition in the subsequent election for the presidency of the ANC in 2012, which the incumbent, President Zuma, won by a handsome majority. The looming vacancy in 2017, however, was a more closely contested race between Cyril Ramaphosa and Nkosazana Dlamini-Zuma, which culminated in Ramaphosa's slim victory. The contest contained an equivalent level of vitriol – it was understood as yet another defining moment in this history of the party – but it was also conducted in a largely orderly manner. The party's national apparatus oversaw the electoral process in an impartial manner, which – in precisely the same way as Polokwane – removed any justification that the loser, Dlamini-Zuma and her supporters, might have had to challenge the result. Richard Calland, in the lead-up to the election, underlined how the central office of the ANC, located in Luthuli House, "have gone out of their way to try to insulate the branch mandates from undue provincial leadership interference, adopting extraordinary measures. This includes having an ANC NEC member present at each branch general meeting".[62]

These episodes in the ANC's recent history underline the core contentions in this article. First, they demonstrate how a canny party leadership empowers the party organization to select public representatives *democratically* – not out of any high-minded commitment to democratic values, but rather because elections are a smart way to stabilize the dominant party. Second, these episodes demonstrate that when the system is calibrated correctly – the party invests in an inclusive selection process, which is underwritten by a neutral party agency to conduct these elections impartially – we see a more orderly form of competition. If, conversely, the components of the system had been out of sync, we would have expected to see a breakdown in the orderliness of these intra-party relationships and a higher potential for conflict, including violent conflict. There was a risk of violence at Polokwane and Johannesburg, but it was neutralized because the losing candidates had neither the justification, nor (apparently) the inclination to contest the validity of the election's outcome.

These episodes at the national level demonstrate the usefulness of the explanatory typology, which outlines how inclusive electoral procedures, and a neutral party agency, stabilize competition between party factions. It is, however, striking that the fierce but orderly competition for national party candidates is not replicated at the sub-national level. This latter category of elections, especially at local level, is equally inclusive, but "political violence", according to von Holdt, "has come to characterize internal conflict over power and access to state resources".[63] This intra-party violence – including the assassination of ANC candidates and representatives – is most prevalent in Mpumalanga and KwaZulu-Natal (KZN); in an ANC investigation into rising levels of violence in the latter province, the party put the number of fatalities at 38 in the period between January 2011 and September 2012.[64] The violence in KZN can be attributed, in part, to the "increasing militarization of the province from the 1980s onwards",[65] but the general factor that explains the higher base level of disorder in local areas can be traced directly to the "lack of a centre of authority in the ANC", which can intervene decisively to regulate the ferocious competition for candidacies and state resources.[66]

Can we reform candidate selection systems to encourage orderly competition?

We get to the heart of the matter now: how, if at all, can we make organizational pre-scriptions that might reduce the level of political disorder inside Africa's dominant political parties? Or, more cynically, how might the leadership of dominant political parties design an "intelligent" system that allows it to redistribute patronage efficiently, maintain its grip on power, and keep good order among its rival constituencies? The critical factor is whether the national party leadership establishes a neutral party agency that acts as a referee, who holds the ring in the contest between rival constituencies for control of the local party machine. If the party leadership is not able to create an apolitical agency on these lines, or commit to a neutral position, it undermines fundamentally the logic of the electoral process – which relies on the "losing" candidate being able to access reliably a "return route" to power. If, conversely, the losing candidate believes that he lost because of illegitimate (or unlawful) interference from the centre of the party, he is more likely to challenge the decision rather than accept his opponent's victory. In a two-party or multi-party system, this unhappy candidate can defect to a rival party, or set up his own party, or perhaps run as an independent candidate – but, in a dominant party system, there are fewer alternative exits in the system.

If, however, the disgruntled candidate cannot reasonably expect to launch a future challenge to return to power, he is more likely to use extra-constitutional – including, *in extremis*, unlawful and even criminal – means to contest the party's decision to nominate a rival. If the stakes are high enough – and they often are when candidates are under enormous pressure to deliver private and club goods to political networks – we can expect, all other things being equal, to see a rise in intra-party violence. The problem with this prescription, obviously, is that it requires myopic elites to cooperate in the short term in order to achieve a long-term pay-off (party cohesion). This kind of cooperation requires trust, which is precisely what is missing in a factional crisis. Still, if donors do engage with political parties, it suggests that they should encourage party leaders to establish a central party agency, beyond partisan control, that can act to maintain the integrity of the party's electoral process.

If the party leadership cannot concede control over the electoral process inside the party, are there other options to consider that might make party competition more orderly, or less prone to violence? I interviewed a leading figure inside the ANC a number of years ago – before the "insurgency" at the party's national conference at Polokwane – who warned, presciently, that "local is not always *lekker* in politics; it can in fact be despotic".[67] It seems obvious, in retrospect, that the openness of ANC procedures enabled a charismatic candidate (Jacob Zuma) to unleash a populist wave of support, which was extremely difficult to regulate (hence the popular description of the campaign as a "Zunami"). Under these circumstances, it might have been better had the procedures not been so inclusive – or, perhaps, *more* inclusive. The genius of the Zuma campaign is that it targeted the branch and regional patrons, who "traded" blocks of support in return for future access to state resources. If the party used a one-member-one-vote formula, it might have been considerably harder for the challenger to use a clientelistic strategy to mobilize such a large base.

The prevalence of violence at the sub-national level highlights a contradiction in the design of the ANC's organization: the party branch is the building block of the party's democratic infrastructure, but it is also the locus of "the insidious internal strife and factional battles for power".[68] The ANC's leadership appreciates that the party must strengthen the organization's "Integrity Commission and dispute resolution mechanisms", but now that the genie is out of the bottle, as it were, it is difficult to see how such a correction, alone, can counteract the ferocious popular pressure to secure access to party candidacies.[69] There is also a dire need to insulate state agencies from party penetration, while empowering law enforcement agencies to investigate impartially and prosecute successfully the perpetrators (and, in particular, the criminal gangs who supply professional assassins), who – in the absence of a credible state commitment to enforce the rule of law – will continue to use violence as a tactical weapon in the battleground of party politics.

Conclusion

What can this case study tell us about how, if at all, we might "craft" a democracy?[70] First, the case underlines how electoral institutions, operating in a context of social diversity and economic inequality, can lead directly to disorderly (and even violent) clientelistic competition for state resources. Von Holdt reaches the dismal but nonetheless compelling conclusion that violence is "inherent" to democratic institutions in this environment.[71] It is, however, unduly pessimistic to imagine that constitutional engineers and party leaders cannot take practical steps to reduce the risk of disorderly competition inside political parties. In this article, I develop a theory that explains both why a dominant party in a divided society is especially prone to outbreaks of violent competition inside its ranks, and how party leaders can design an organizational apparatus to reduce this risk. There is no panacea, of course, but there are concrete steps that can be implemented to stabilize competition.

This case also provides a theoretical insight into the anatomy of a dominant party. If the political party is indispensable to a democracy, it is also dangerous: the party is a powerful instrument that elites can manipulate to undermine the public interest. If this axiom applies to all political parties, it applies doubly to the dominant political party – not simply because it has an in-built majority, or tends to degenerate into a clientelistic "machine", but also because its endogenization of social conflict makes it especially prone to disorder inside its ranks. This vulnerability places an onus on party leaders to design an organization to regulate this conflict in an orderly way. The stand-out conclusion of the experience of the ANC in South Africa suggests that an electoral mechanism can produce orderly competition, *only if* the party invests in an organization that applies impartially the rules governing the election.

Finally, this case highlights an important continuity in the political development of postcolonial states: the new and insecure leadership – operating in the space between a divided society and weak state – must make a choice about how to govern authoritatively. If the new leadership empowers the political party to act as a vehicle to regulate social competition for state resources, it opens up an institutional space to stabilize the regime – but this strategy also displaces competition from the public arena to the partisan organization. It is a risky manoeuvre to perform in *any* context; it is especially risky in a divided and unequal society. If venal elites use elections to capture the organization, the dominant party – irrespective of whether elections are conducted in an orderly manner – can be transformed into an instrument to penetrate, strip and ultimately weaken the state institutions of a new and fragile democracy.

Notes

1. Candidate selection is "the predominately extralegal process by which a political party decides which of the persons legally eligible to hold an elective public office will be designated on the ballot and in elections communication as its recommended and supported candidate or list of candidates" (Ranney, "Candidate Selection," 75).
2. I consider a party system to be "dominant" when one party manages to win an absolute majority of seats in parliament, and exercises control over the political executive, over at least three consecutive elections. For a detailed discussion on how to define dominance, see Bogaards, "Counting Parties and Identifying Dominant Party Systems in Africa." For a detailed discussion on how to define different types of candidate selection system, see Rahat and Hazan, "Candidate Selection Methods."
3. Carothers, *Confronting the Weakest Link*, 6–7; Mainwaring, *Rethinking Party Systems in the Third Wave of Democratization*, 3–14.
4. Van de Walle and Butler, "Political Parties and Party Systems in Africa's Illiberal Democracies"; Bogaards, "Counting Parties and Identifying Dominant Party Systems in Africa."
5. Mozaffar, Scarritt, and Galaich, "Electoral Institutions, Ethnopolitical Cleavages, and Party Systems in Africa's Emerging Democracies"; Brambor, Clark, and Golder, "Are African Party Systems Different?"; Lindberg, "Consequences of Electoral Systems in Africa."
6. Kuenzi and Lambright, "Party System Institutionalization in 30 African Countries"; Lindberg, "Institutionalization of Party Systems?"; Manning, "Assessing African Party Systems After the Third Wave"; Mozaffar and Scarritt, "The Puzzle of African Party Systems."
7. Wahman, "Nationalized Incumbents and Regional Challengers."
8. Basedau et al., "Ethnicity and Party Preference in Sub-Saharan Africa."
9. Gunther and Diamond, "A New Typology."
10. Elischer, *Political Parties in Africa.*
11. Carothers, *Confronting the Weakest Link*, 6–7.
12. On this classification of Africa's political parties, see Gunther and Diamond, "A New Typology."
13. This kind of clientelistic competition also creates a severe long-term problem: it demolishes the party's moral claim to govern in the public interest. See Mac Giollabhuí, "The Fall of an African President."
14. Allen, "Understanding African Politics."
15. Jackson and Rosberg, "Why Africa's Weak States Persist," 1–24.
16. Mamdani, *Citizen and Subject.*
17. Migdal, *Strong Societies and Weak States.*
18. Bienen, *One-Party Systems in Africa*, 109.
19. Coleman and Rosberg, "Conclusions," 663.
20. Zolberg, *Creating Political Order*, 41.
21. Lemarchand "Political Clientelism and Ethnicity in Tropical Africa."
22. Zolberg, *Creating Political Order*, 42.
23. Coleman and Rosberg, "Conclusions," 668.
24. Ibid., 656.
25. This dilemma was not unique to Africa. In authoritarian Spain during the 1960s, Huntington describes how "the Franco regime was caught in a dilemma. If such political participation were channelled into the Falange, it would disrupt the balance within the regime. But if it were not absorbed into some element of the regime, it would eventually threaten the system itself." Huntington, "Social and Institutional Dynamics of One-Party Systems."
26. This strategic decision to demobilize political institutions has had a long-term and deleterious effect on politics in Africa (see Wanyama and Elklit 2018). On how the suppression of a *corps intermédiares* eradicated viable alternatives to ethnic parties, see Lebas, *From Parties to Protest*; and Coleman and Rosberg, "Conclusions," 670.
27. Coleman and Rosberg, "Conclusions," 670.
28. Apter "Parties and National Integration in Africa," 269.
29. Gertzel and Szeftel, *The Dynamics of the One-Party State in Africa*, 102.
30. Van de Walle, *The Politics of Permanent Crisis.*
31. Cheeseman, "Nationalism, the One-Party State, and Military Rule," 15.
32. For the original statement on how political parties assumed the characteristics of a "machine", see Zolberg, *Creating Political Order*. Roger Southall extends Zolberg's thesis to southern Africa,

documenting how liberation movements have become "a machine for the allocation of positions, privileges, resources, and contracts", *Liberation Movements in Power*, 16.

33. A party that experiences a (negative) change in its cohesion suffers from a high level of resignations, defections, splits and, in the worst case, the complete breakdown or collapse of the party. A cohesive party is not necessarily highly "orderly." See Seeberg et al., 2018, for a definition of varying degrees of disorder that mark contests to select candidates.
34. Randall and Svåsand, "Party Institutionalization in New Democracies," 12.
35. Panebianco, *Political Parties*, 32.
36. Huntington, "Social and Institutional Dynamics of One-Party Systems," 31–32.
37. Aldrich, *Why Parties?*
38. Gallagher, "Introduction." See, also, Rahat and Hazan, "Candidate Selection Methods."
39. Shugart, "Comparative Electoral Systems Research," 38.
40. For an excellent review of this literature, see Brancati, "Democratic Authoritarianism."
41. Geddes, "What Do We Know About Democratization."
42. Gandhi and Lust-Okar, "Elections Under Authoritarianism."
43. See Mac Giollabhuí, "How Things Fall Apart."
44. Using the least squares index of disproportionality, South Africa has an average score of 0.33. On the calculation of this index, see Gallagher and Mitchell, "Appendix C," 621.
45. Interview with ANC MP, September 2012.
46. Butler, "How Democratic is the African National Congress?," 726.
47. Bond, "In Power in Pretoria?," 87.
48. Von Holdt, "South Africa," 591.
49. On South African exceptionalism, see Mamdani, *Citizen and Subject*, 27.
50. ANC, *Organizational Renewal*, 18–21.
51. Suttner, cited in Southall, "Understanding the 'Zuma Tsunami'," 327.
52. Lodge, "The ANC and the Development of Party Politics in Modern South Africa," 213.
53. Beresford, "Power, Patronage, and Gatekeeper Politics in South Africa," 237.
54. Southall, "Democracy at Risk?," 59
55. ANC, *Organizational Renewal*, 14.
56. Huntington, *Political Order in Changing Societies*, 461.
57. Interview with ANC MP, September 2011
58. Interview with ANC MP, September 2012.
59. For a more detailed account of Jacob Zuma's victory at Polokwane, see Mac Giollabhuí, "The Fall of an African President."
60. Chikane, *Eight Days in September*, 155.
61. Interview with ANC MP, August 2011.
62. Calland, "Cyril Ramaphosa Leads, But Foul Play May Snatch Victory."
63. Von Holdt, "South Africa," 597.
64. Bruce, "A Provincial Concern?," 15.
65. Taylor, *Justice Denied*, 24.
66. Von Holdt, "South Africa," 598.
67. Interview with Kader Asmal, December 2005.
68. ANC, "Organizational Renewal and Organizational Design," 15.
69. Ibid., 25.
70. Di Palma, *To Craft Democracies*.
71. Von Holdt, "South Africa," 602.

Disclosure statement

No potential conflict of interest was reported by the author.

Bibliography

African National Congress. "Organizational Renewal and Organizational Design: Discussion Document." 5th National Policy Conference of the ANC, 2017. http://www.anc.org.za/sites/default/files/National%20Policy%20Conference%202017%20Organisational%20Renewal.pdf.

Aldrich, J. H. *Why Parties? The Origin and Transformation of Political Parties in America.* Chicago: University of Chicago Press, 1995.

Allen, C. "Understanding African Politics." *Review of African Political Economy* 22, no. 65 (1995): 301–320.

Apter, David. "Ghana" In *Political Parties and National Integration in Tropical Africa*, edited by James S. Coleman, and Carl G. Rosberg. Berkeley: University of California Press, 1966.

Basedau, M., G. Erdmann, J. Lay, and A. Stroh. "Ethnicity and Party Preference in Sub-Saharan Africa." *Democratization* 18, no. 2 (2011): 462–489.

Beresford, A. "Power, Patronage, and Gatekeeper Politics in South Africa." *African Affairs* 114, no. 455 (2015): 226–248.

Bienen, H. *One-Party Systems in Africa.* Princeton, NJ: Princeton University Press, 1968.

Bogaards, M. "Counting Parties and Identifying Dominant Party Systems in Africa." *European Journal of Political Research* 43, no. 2 (2004): 173–197.

Bond, P. "In Power in Pretoria? Reply to R.W. Johnson." *New Left Review* 58 (2009): 77–88.

Brambor, T., W. R. Clark, and M. Golder. "Are African Party Systems Different?" *Electoral Studies* 26, no. 2 (2007): 315–323.

Brancati, D. "Democratic Authoritarianism: Origins and Effects." *Annual Review of Political Science* 17 (2014): 313–326.

Bruce, D. "A Provincial Concern? Political Killings in South Africa." *SA Crime Quarterly* 45, no. 3 (2013): 13–23.

Butler, A. "How Democratic is the African National Congress?" *Journal of Southern African Studies* 31, no. 4 (2005): 719–736.

Calland, R. "Cyril Ramaphosa Leads, But Foul Play May Snatch Victory," *Mail and Guardian*, November 23, 2017. https://mg.co.za/article/2017-11-23-cyril-ramaphosa-leads-but-foul-play-may-snatch-victory

Carothers, T. *Confronting the Weakest Link: Aiding Political Parties in New Democracies.* Washington, DC: Carnegie Endowment for International Peace, 2006.

Cheeseman, Nic. "Nationalism, the One-Party State, and Military Rule" In *The Routledge Handbook of African Politics*, edited by Nic Cheeseman, David Anderson, and Andrea Scheibler. Abingdon: Routledge, 2013.

Chikane, F. *Eight Days in September: The Removal of Thabo Mbeki.* Johannesburg: Picador Africa, 2012.

Coleman, J. S., and C. G. Rosberg. "Conclusions." In *Political Parties and National Integration in Tropical Africa*, edited by J. S. Coleman, and Carl G. Rosberg, 655–692. Berkeley: University of California Press, 1964.

Di Palma, G. *To Craft Democracies: An Essay on Democratic Transitions.* Berkeley: University of California Press, 1990.

Elischer, S. *Political Parties in Africa: Ethnicity and Party Formation.* Cambridge: Cambridge University Press, 2013.

Gallagher, M. "Introduction." In *Candidate Selection in Comparative Perspective*, edited by Michael Gallagher, and Michael Marsh, 1–19. London: Sage, 1988.

Gallagher, M., and P. Mitchell. "Appendix C." In *The Politics of Electoral Systems*, 607–621. Oxford: Oxford University Press, 2005.

Gandhi, J., and E. Lust-Okar. "Elections Under Authoritarianism." *Annual Review of Political Science* 12 (2009): 403–422.

Geddes, B. "What Do We Know About Democratization After Twenty Years?" *Annual Review of Political Science* 2, no. 1 (1999): 115–144.

Gertzel, C. J., and M. Szeftel. *The Dynamics of the One-Party State in Zambia.* Manchester: Manchester University Press, 1984.

Gunther, R., and L. Diamond. "Species of Political Parties: A New Typology." *Party Politics* 9, no. 2 (2003): 167–199.

Huntington, S. P. *Political Order in Changing Societies.* New Haven, CT: Yale University Press, 1968.

Huntington, S. P. "Social and Institutional Dynamics of One-Party Systems." In *Authoritarian Politics in Modern Society: The Dynamics of Established One-Party Systems*, edited by Samuel P. Huntington, and Clement Henry Moore, 15–35. Basic Books: New York, 1970

Jackson, R. H., and C. G. Rosberg. "Why Africa's Weak States Persist: The Empirical and the Juridical in Statehood." *World Politics* 35, no. 1 (1982): 1–24.

Kothari, R. "The Congress System in India." *Asian Survey* 4, no. 12 (1964): 1161–1173.

Kuenzi, M., and G. Lambright. "Party System Institutionalization in 30 African Countries." *Party Politics* 7, no. 4 (2001): 437–468.

LeBas, A. *From Protest to Parties: Party-Building and Democratization in Africa.* Oxford: Oxford University Press, 2013.

Lemarchand, R. "Political Clientelism and Ethnicity in Tropical Africa: Competing Solidarities in Nation Building." *American Political Science Review* 66, no. 1 (1972): 68–90.

Lindberg, S. "Consequences of Electoral Systems in Africa: A Preliminary Inquiry." *Electoral Studies* 24, no. 1 (2005): 41–64.

Lindberg, S. "Institutionalization of Party Systems? Stability and Fluidity among Legislative Parties in Africa's Democracies." *Government and Opposition* 42, no. 2 (2007): 215–241.

Lodge, T. "The ANC and the Development of Party Politics in Modern South Africa." *The Journal of Modern African Studies* 42, no. 2 (2004): 189–219.

Mac Giollabhuí, S. "The Fall of an African President: How and Why Did the ANC Unseat Thabo Mbeki?" *African Affairs* 116, no. 464 (2017): 1–23.

Mac Giollabhuí, S. "How Things Fall Apart: Candidate Selection and the Cohesion of Dominant Parties in South Africa and Namibia." *Party Politics* 19, no. 4 (2013): 577–600.

Mainwaring, S. *Rethinking Party Systems in the Third Wave of Democratization: The Case of Brazil.* Stanford, CA: Stanford University Press, 1999.

Mamdani, M. *Citizen and Subject: Contemporary Africa and the Legacy of Late Colonialism.* Princeton, NJ: Princeton University Press, 1996.

Manning, C. "Assessing African Party Systems After the Third Wave." *Party Politics* 11, no. 6 (2005): 707–727.

Migdal, J. S. *Strong Societies and Weak States: State-Society Relations and State Capabilities in the Third World.* Princeton, NJ: Princeton University Press, 1988.

Mozaffar, S., and J. R. Scarritt. "The Puzzle of African Party Systems." *Party Politics* 11, no. 4 (2005): 399–421.

Mozaffar, S., J. R. Scarritt, and G. Galaich. "Electoral Institutions, Ethnopolitical Cleavages, and Party Systems in Africa's Emerging Democracies." *American Political Science Review* 97, no. 3 (2003): 379–390.

Panebianco, A. *Political Parties: Organization and Power.* Cambridge: Cambridge University Press, 1988.

Rahat, G., and R. Hazan. "Candidate Selection Methods an Analytical Framework." *Party Politics* 7, no. 3 (2001): 297–322.

Randall, V., and L. Svåsand. "Party Institutionalization in New Democracies." *Party Politics* 8, no. 1 (2002): 5–29.

Ranney, A. "Candidate Selection." In *Democracy at the Polls*, edited by David Butler, Howard R. Penniman, and Austin Ranney, 63–82. Washington, DC: American Enterprise Institute, 1981.

Shugart, M. S. "Comparative Electoral Systems Research: The Maturation of a Field." In *The Politics of Electoral Systems*, edited by Michael Gallagher, and Paul Mitchell, 25–57. Oxford: Oxford University Press, 2005.

Southall, R. "Democracy at Risk? Politics and Governance Under the ANC." *The ANNALS of the American Academy of Political and Social Science* 652, no. 1 (2014): 48–69.

Southall, R. *Liberation Movements in Power: Party and State in Southern Africa.* Woodbridge, Suffolk: James Currey, 2013.

Southall, R. "Understanding the 'Zuma Tsunami'." *Review of African Political Economy* 36, no. 121 (2009): 317–333.

Taylor, R. *Justice Denied: Political Violence in KwaZulu-Natal After 1994.* Johannesburg: Centre for the Study of Violence and Reconciliation, 2002.

Van de Walle, N. *The Politics of Permanent Crisis.* Cambridge: Cambridge University Press, 2001.

Van de Walle, N., and K. S. Butler. "Political Parties and Party Systems in Africa's Illiberal Democracies." *Cambridge Review of International Affairs* 13, no. 1 (1999): 14–28.

Von Holdt, K. ""South Africa: The Transition to Violent Democracy"." *Review of African Political Economy* 40, no. 138 (2013): 589–604.

Wahman, M. "Nationalized Incumbents and Regional Challengers Opposition- and Incumbent-Party Nationalization in Africa." *Party Politics* 23, no. 3 (2017): 309–322.

Zolberg, A. *Creating Political Order. The Party States of West Africa.* Chicago: Rand McNally & Company, 1966.

Fighting for a name on the ballot: constituency-level analysis of nomination violence in Zambia

Edward Goldring and Michael Wahman

ABSTRACT
What factors increase the likelihood of nomination violence? Nomination violence can be an expression of both horizontal conflict, between local political elites, and vertical conflict, between national and local elites. We theorize about factors that may increase the risks of vertical and horizontal conflict and leverage a unique dataset of constituency-level nomination violence obtained from surveys with 464 domestic election observers active in the 2016 Zambian general election. Our statistical analyses show constituencies with an incumbent standing for re-election were more likely to experience nomination violence. Also, contrary to previous research on general election violence, we theorize and find that more rural constituencies had a higher propensity for nomination violence than urban constituencies. Our findings highlight the importance of intra-party power relations and the bargaining relationship between the centre and periphery.

In the recent 2016 South African local elections, riots erupted in a Pretoria suburb due to internal quarrels in the African National Congress (ANC) over the city's mayoral nominations. In the riots, supporters of the incumbent mayor set buildings on fire as a protest against the party's adoption of a rival mayoral candidate.[1] In a similar incident in Malawi's 2014 election, violence erupted between supporters of the People's Party in Karonga Central constituency. Supporters of former Member of Parliament (MP) Frank Mwenifumbo vandalized property and blocked roads, alleging that the Deputy Minister of Finance, Cornelius Mwalwanda, stole the vote.[2] Despite a recent surge in research on election violence, particularly in Africa,[3] we are poorly equipped to explain these examples from South Africa and Malawi. Most systematic research on election violence in Africa has been confined to the general election stage, with little or no reference to violence occurring during the nomination of candidates. Our truncated understanding of the African electoral process limits our comprehension of contemporary African democracy. Although violence at the nomination stage is not always as widespread or as large-scale as violence at later stages of the electoral cycle, nominations that fail to meet acceptable democratic standards may distort electoral legitimacy even before the start of national general election campaigns and may initiate an escalating cycle of electoral violence.

ⓑ Supplemental data for this article can be accessed at https://doi.org/10.1080/13510347.2017.1394844

Given prevailing polarization of geographic voting patterns in most of Africa,[4] violence during nominations may seem unsurprising. Most African electoral systems exhibit low levels of competition at the local level. As a consequence, party nominations become high-stakes competitions. Nominations may result in two forms of conflict: horizontal and vertical. Horizontal conflict refers to conflict between local elites vying for political office as low inter-party competition moves the focus from general elections to nominations. Vertical conflict refers to conflict between local and national political interests. For national elites, nominations are important in crafting national coalitions. However, the interests of national elites are not always aligned with local preferences, which results in vertical conflict. These horizontal and vertical conflicts are frequently decided in an inadequate institutional framework, free from real transparency and lacking in democratic legitimacy.

In this study, we offer three main contributions. First, we shine a spotlight on subnational variations in nomination violence and provide a theoretical framework for the occurrence of nomination violence. Violence in local primaries deserves to be studied in more detail in parallel to, but also separately from, election violence in general election campaigns.

Second, we employ an innovative sub-national research design based on expert interviews with domestic election monitors. Through this approach, we leverage constituency-level data on nomination violence from the Zambian 2016 general election to study the local political dynamics conducive to nomination violence. Zambia is a typical case of African nominations where nomination procedures are carried out consistently across constituencies and parties. It is also a case that, as of lately, occupies the African middle ground in relation to election violence.[5] Violence is a prominent feature of elections but we still have important subnational variations. Although existing cross-national work on election violence[6] has been useful to develop better understanding of dynamics leading to violence in elections, cross-national studies may give rise to important ecological fallacies. When aggregating political, economic, and social variables (such as competition or ethnic polarization) to the national level, we risk estimating conditions that do not accurately depict political conditions in local environments where elections actually take place.

Third, we offer an inventory of factors that may increase the risk of horizontal or vertical conflict. We look particularly at the effect of inter-party competition, intra-party competition, intra-party democracy, and local bargaining power vis-à-vis the centre. Our statistical analyses of all 156 constituencies in the 2016 Zambian election show strong support for the intra-party competition and bargaining power hypotheses. In constituencies where an incumbent MP tries to re-secure the party's nomination, the probability of nomination violence is significantly lower than in constituencies where the incumbent MP does not participate in nominations, particularly if the incumbent represents the ruling party. The existence of an incumbent MP reduces horizontal uncertainty by providing a clear front-runner. Furthermore, contrary to previous studies finding urban localities are more prone to election violence,[7] we find constituencies with lower population density are significantly more likely to experience nomination violence. These constituencies are more likely to be within the periphery of the internal power structures and have lower bargaining power vis-à-vis the centre.

Nomination violence and subnational variations

Nomination violence is best understood as a subset of the broader category of election violence.[8] Following the introductory article of this special issue, we understand nomination violence as either a threat or an actual act of violence against a voter, candidate, government official, or property during the nomination phase, with the ambition to influence the electoral process or outcome.[9] Such violence is often, but not per definition, intra-party violence.

Nomination violence can serve many possible purposes. It can be used as a form of intimidation or coercion against candidates or voters in nominations and be an expression of horizontal conflict between aspiring candidates and conflicting local interests. It may also be a way for losing candidates to signal strength for upcoming elections, particularly if their plan is to defect and mount a new challenge on an independent or alternative party ticket.

However, horizontal conflict is not the only form of conflict that may be conducive to violence. Conflict may also be vertical, where violence is a manifestation of conflict between central party hierarchies and local party branches. This type of violence will often be used to protest the adoption of locally unpopular candidates and can result in damage of government or party property or violence against state and party officials. Poorly institutionalized procedures create ambiguities in nomination procedures and tend to exacerbate conflicts between the interests of central party organizations and local chapters. African political parties, especially those in power, tend to be loosely tied coalitions of diverse local interests. Central party organizations offer access to central economic and political resources in exchange for local access to clientelistic networks.[10] Decentralized nominations fulfil an important role in giving local power brokers input into the political affairs of the party. Moreover, nominations create a venue for power brokers to extract rents from prospective candidates.[11] However, candidate selection presents a delicate bargain between the centre and the periphery where the centre's decision to override local preferences has the potential to stir violence.

The propensity for vertical and horizontal conflict varies between, but also within, countries. Depending on a sub-national political unit's internal political dynamics and the unit's relationship to the centre, a sub-national unit should be more or less prone to nomination violence. In this way, nomination violence like general election violence should not be equally spread across space.[12] However, environments conducive to violence in the nomination phase are not necessarily the same as the ones prone to violence in general elections. For the actors involved, the sources and levels of competition and electoral considerations change over the course of the electoral cycle. This study offers an inventory of four hypotheses of nomination violence: inter-party competition, intra-party competition, intra-party democracy, and bargaining position vis-à-vis the centre. These hypotheses are not intended as mutually exclusive; rather, they posit different mechanisms for the occurrence of nomination violence. Also, the idea of both horizontal and vertical conflict will not relate to all of our individual hypotheses presented below. Instead, this is meant to work as a framework from which we can start theorizing about sub-national variations in nomination violence.

Inter-party competition

In the general literature on election violence, it is often hypothesized that high levels of inter-party competition are conducive to violence.[13] Violence is costly for both candidates and perpetrators; political actors are normally not prepared to incur the cost of engaging in violence unless electoral outcomes are uncertain. However, the dynamics change drastically between general election violence and nomination violence. In the nomination phase we expect low inter-party competition would be conducive to violence as it exacerbates the risk of horizontal conflict. Indeed, reports of violence in nominations have surrounded several nationally dominant parties such as Uganda's National Resistance Movement and the ANC in South Africa.[14]

When parties are locally dominant, general elections are of little consequence. Whoever clinches the locally dominant party's ticket is likely to become the eventual MP. In constituencies where inter-party competition is low, the fiercest competition will therefore be within rather than between parties. Writing about the highly polarized Ghanaian elections, where few constituencies swing back and forth between the two major parties, both Lindberg and Ichino and Nathan remark how bribery, which is not a form of violence but certainly a form of manipulation, has become a prominent feature of primary elections.[15] Moreover, when political success becomes hard to achieve outside the dominant party, diverse groups within the community with varying interests are likely to compete within the same party. The above dynamics are likely to increase horizontal conflict within constituencies and move conflict from the campaign period to the nomination period. We therefore hypothesize:

H₁: Constituencies with low levels of inter-party competition have a higher probability of nomination violence.

Intra-party competition

Political parties in Africa have mostly remained weak throughout the post-colonial era. The organizational capacity of political parties in countries like Zambia, particularly in the geographical peripheries, is limited. The colonial state compensated for its lack of control in the rural hinterlands by creating a system of indirect rule.[16] Similarly, African parties after independence, both during one-partyism and multi-partyism, often allowed for a system of "pre-bendalism", where local elites were brought into the party coalition by a system that used public offices for personal access to state resources.[17] The resulting system has been a symbiotic relationship between political parties and local elites where local dominance is not only party dominance but also *personal dominance* as political spaces are controlled by local political strongmen.

Instigating primary violence against the likely party nominee is costly and futile. Candidates and voters who engage in violence against the supporters of a likely nominee would expect retaliation and would likely be left out of the winning coalition after an eventual general election victory. Thus, without high intra party competition there are few incentives to engage in violence. Whereas in constituencies where competition within the party is more open and the outcome uncertain, violence may be a more viable strategy both as a tool to show local strength and to protest after decisions are made by the national executive committee.

Personal dominance that reduces intra-party competition could come from several sources. Local candidates with strong connections to other local elites, such as chiefs and business interests, should be in a strong position against other intra-party rivals.[18] In addition, constituencies where one candidate controls significantly more economic resources than his/her competitors should have lower levels of intra-party competition. One easily observable indicator of low intra-party competition is incumbency. Although incumbent MPs are not certain to win nominations,[19] incumbent candidates should have several advantages vis-à-vis their intra-party rivals. Access to political office provides incumbents with economic resources usually not accessible to non-incumbent candidates. During their time in parliament, incumbent MPs can create a strong local patronage network to strengthen their support during nomination procedures. Equally, or even more importantly, incumbent MPs serve as a bridge between national and local elites, hence, mitigating vertical conflicts. We therefore hypothesize:

> H_2: Constituencies with an incumbent MP contesting the nomination have a lower probability of nomination violence.

Intra-party democracy

Parts of the research on electoral manipulation and election violence emphasize how violations of the electoral code of conduct are likely to reduce the legitimacy of the electoral process and enable violence.[20] Most importantly, when manipulation is overt during the election campaign it increases the risks for post-election protest and violence as disgruntled losers have reasons to challenge the legitimacy of the results.[21]

Similar to electoral laws in general elections, political parties' internal regulations pertaining to nomination procedures are followed to a varying extent. Adherence to these rules and regulations can vary across, potentially undermining democratic norms in certain constituencies. African parties have often been criticized for their top-down organization and lack of internal democracy. Indeed, Western party assistance organizations have devoted considerable resources to strengthening party constitutions and inclusion.[22]

The use and application of rules shows the asymmetric power relations between the centre and the periphery, where central party organizations are free to delegate as much or as little power to local branches as they see fit. The opaque and irregular application of rules often leads to vertical conflict between articulated local interests and central party organizations that decide to neglect the preferences of local branches. Such conflict has the potential to escalate into violence. We therefore hypothesize:

> H_3: Constituencies where central party organizations neglect local preferences have a higher probability of nomination violence.

Bargaining power vis-à-vis the centre

Violence during elections has often been primarily associated with urban spaces. Studying Côte Ivoire, Straus found that much of the violence in the 2010 election was concentrated in urban areas.[23] Similarly, Dercon and Guitérrez-Romero found that urban Kenyans were significantly more likely to have been exposed to violence in the 2007 election than their rural compatriots.[24] Urban localities have a wealth of possible perpetrators of violence and grant more anonymity to those engaging in violent behaviour. However, nomination violence is likely to work rather differently than general election violence, at least in cases where the selectorate is small (when nominations fall short of an open primary). In nominations, violence is more likely to be a form of protest rather than a tool to deter turnout. Nominations represent a delicate bargain between the party centre and the rural periphery. The centre solicits local elites for advice, but may ultimately decide not to follow local preferences. As remote, rural areas are further removed from the centre of power, they are more likely to be in conflict with the interests of the central elites. Central party elites would also be more inclined to circumvent the interests of local elites in rural areas; such elites will be of less national importance. This could also lead to increased vertical conflict as local elites will perceive that counter-elites, even incumbents, are less protected by national party structures and, hence, these seats are more up for grabs. Indeed, looking at nominations for the United National Independence Party (UNIP) in the 1973 one-party elections, Baylies and Szeftel showed that Lusaka was the only region where UNIP did not disqualify any candidates.[25] Boone made the argument that local African elites in the poorest most rural areas have had the lowest bargaining power throughout the colonial and post-colonial era.[26] Weaker rural elites are more likely to be sidelined in the adaptation of candidates, hence causing vertical conflict. The final hypothesis is therefore:

H_4: *More rural constituencies have a higher probability of nomination violence.*

Party nominations and violence in Zambia

Zambia represents a typical case of an African competitive authoritarian regime.[27] Elections feature high levels of competition and significant uncertainty, at least at the central level. However, electoral procedures are poorly institutionalized and manipulation, both at the local and national level, is systematic.[28] Despite high levels of national competition, Zambia has lately become hugely polarized between a "Green" east, controlled by the incumbent Patriotic Front (PF), and a "Red" west controlled by the opposition United Party for National Development (UPND) (see Figure 1). Parliamentary elections are held in Single Member District (SMD) elections and in 2016 most victories fell along predictable party lines. The low level of local inter-party competitiveness created a situation where nominations were crucial for eventual distribution of power.

Zambia is also a fairly typical African case in relation to party nomination procedures. The main Zambian parties have settled for remarkably similar nomination rules. Although there have been attempts to institutionalize nomination procedures and increase inclusiveness compared to earlier elections,[29] nomination procedures fall somewhere in the middle of the decentralization spectrum.[30] Both the PF and UPND had significant local input in the selection process, but fell short of full decentralization. Political parties advertised for interested candidates to file an application with their local constituency branches. Interested candidates were later interviewed by their ward, constituency, district, and province party committees. Each level voted on their preferred ranking of candidates before the list was passed upward in the party hierarchy. PF committees at the constituency, district, and province levels consisted of several representatives from each wing of the party: the main wing, the women's wing, and the youth wing. The UPND committees were similar, but also allowed input from so-called "trustees" of the party, who could be local notables. The number of committee members at each level varied from a dozen to a couple of hundred. Eventually, provincial committees made a recommendation to the Party's National Executive Committee (NEC) and ranked the top candidates.[31] The NEC had the right to follow the recommendation from the provincial committee or nominate a different candidate.

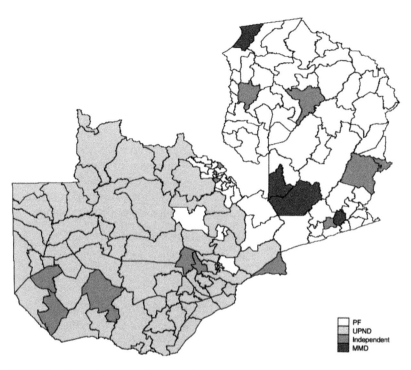

Figure 1. 2016 Zambian parliamentary election results.

Studying nominations in Ghana, Ichino and Nathan argue primaries can be used to mitigate distributional conflicts between central and local party leadership.[32] Decentralized primaries create opportunities for local party members to extract rent from local candidates. Nomination procedures in Zambia seem to have performed a similar function. Several reports of corruption in nominations surfaced during the election cycle and civil society organizations expressed concerns about the conduct of nominations.[33] However, although nominations created opportunities for local rent-seeking, central party elites did not relinquish their ultimate right of nomination decisions. The opaque process frequently created vertical conflict between the centre and periphery, putting preferential differences on open display. In fact, the manifestation of vertical conflict in nominations has been a constant in Zambian politics. Rakner and Svåsand describe how local branches of the opposition party Forum for Democracy and Development objected to the parachuting of senior officials into safe seats in the 2001 election.[34] However, vertical conflicts in nominations actually pre-date the introduction to multi-partyism. For the 1973 and 1978 one-party UNIP elections, the ruling party designed a system with both local and central input in arriving at the three UNIP candidates presented to voters in the general election. As the national party organization interfered with local primaries to promote specifically powerful elites, conflict between the centre and the periphery was known to occur.[35]

The rather complex system of nominations in the 2016 election created significant confusion, not least because both political parties also kept an eye on the other party's nominations with the intention to possibly pick up candidates who did not clinch the nomination in the rival party. In many instances, parties ended up nominating candidates who never formally applied, applied for another party but were unsuccessful, or who applied for the same party in a different constituency but were unsuccessful. The procedures were further complicated by the new constitution's rather ambiguous academic qualification criteria that made certain candidates unqualified to stand for office. In some constituencies, parties even issued adoption certificates to two or more candidates creating considerable confusion.[36]

Our data found nomination violence in 18 constituencies, or about 12% of the total.[37] The number may seem rather small, but violence was the tip of the iceberg of a largely conflictual nomination process. Figure 2 shows the location of constituencies with nomination violence. The severity of the violence varied somewhat, but in all but one case where we recorded violence, it was violence directed towards people.[38] No fatalities were recorded, but three cases had injuries. Violence in cases like Chongwe and Ndola Central was recorded after results were announced as a way to protest against the procedures. In Livingstone, violence erupted within the UPND between supporters of Matthews Jere and Joseph Akafumba. Both candidates had been issued nomination certificates and supporters of Akafumba attempted to block Jere from filing his nomination with the electoral commission.[39]

It may also be worth comparing frequency and severity of violence in the Zambian case in the nomination process, during the general campaign, and after election day.

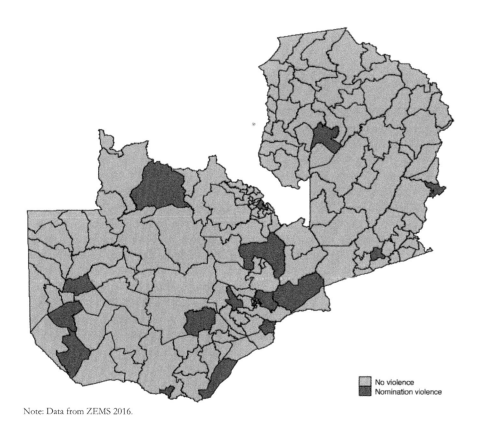

No violence
Nomination violence

Note: Data from ZEMS 2016.

Figure 2. Nomination violence in the 2016 Zambian elections.
Note: Data from ZEMS 2016.

Table 1. Frequency and severity of Zambian election violence by number and percentage of constituencies across different stages of the electoral cycle.

	Violence without injuries or serious property damage	Violence with serious property damage	Violence with injuries or fatalities
Nomination	15 (10%)	0 (0%)	3 (2%)
Campaign period	41 (26%)	2 (1%)	22 (14%)
Post-election period	17 (11%)	8 (5%)	9 (6%)

Note: Data from ZEMS 2016.

Although this article focuses particularly on nomination violence, our survey (described below) also included questions regarding violence at other times of the electoral cycle. Table 1 shows the difference between the three stages. We divide constituencies here between those that had violence without serious property damage or injuries, those that had serious property damage, and those that had injuries.[40] Violence was less frequent and generally less severe in the nomination phase. However, even this low-intensity violence can have adverse effects on the democratic process, not least in systems such as Zambia, where losing primary candidates go on to contest general elections on alternative party tickets or as independents. These descriptive data help us put nomination violence in perspective, although we would be reluctant to generalize findings about frequency of different forms (nomination/pre/post) of violence outside the Zambian context. For instance, as argued by Kjaer in this issue, cases like Uganda actually had higher levels of violence at the nomination stage than at later stages of the electoral cycle.

Data

We test the hypotheses with original constituency-level election violence data from the 2016 general election. Variables are measured using the Zambia Election Monitor Survey (ZEMS). ZEMS is a post-election survey conducted with 464 domestic election observers in the month after the Zambian elections.[41] ZEMS respondents were drawn from domestic election observers from the Foundation for Democratic Process (FODEP) and the Southern African Center for Constructive Resolution of Disputes (SACCORD). Both FODEP and SACCORD are non-partisan civil society organizations with support from the international donor community. In the election, they split the monitoring of Zambia's 156 constituencies between them. FODEP monitored 96 constituencies, and SACCORD oversaw 60. FODEP deployed 5000 monitors, while SACCORD deployed 4000.

ZEMS survey respondents were recruited as non-biased experts, with the assistance of FODEP and SACCORD's executive directors. We liaised with FODEP and SACCORD to secure respondents with relevant monitor training, a clear awareness of the entire electoral cycle in their respective constituency, and no known partisan bias. Respondents were intentionally not a random sample, and comprised a sample of experts, similar to other expert surveys on election integrity.[42] Institutionally, FODEP and SACCORD are non-partisan, so there is no reason to suspect systematic partisan bias in reporting. Regarding individual respondents, any prospective bias should be alleviated by the fact that multiple respondents were surveyed for each constituency (see further discussion below). Interviews with respondents were conducted via phone in English or one of the main local languages: Bemba, Lozi, Nyanja, and Tonga.

The expert survey approach used to capture nomination violence sub-nationally has several benefits compared to other data used in previous studies, particularly compared to event data from media reports. Earlier research has used event data from sources such as the Social Conflict Analysis Database (SCAD) and the Armed Conflict Location and Event Data Project (ACLED) to measure election violence sub-nationally.[43] However, such research has shown a significant urban bias in the reporting of violence.[44]

Dependent variable and model specification

The outcome of interest is nomination election violence for the 2016 Zambia tripartite elections. ZEMS asked respondents whether any violence occurred during the nomination period in their constituency. We define nomination violence as violence relating to the nominations prior to candidates filing their nomination papers and thus becoming the candidate for a particular party, or as an independent, as well as election violence related to the nominations after a candidate has been selected. For example, the latter could include fights after the deadline for candidates to file their nomination papers on 31 May 2016, if it was between factions of a party about the identity of the chosen candidate.

Respondents in each constituency were asked whether there were any reports of nomination violence. Additionally, respondents either voluntarily provided, or were prompted to provide, details about incidents if they said violence occurred. As the above definition is quite flexible, it ensures that we capture nomination violence. Respondents frequently provided rich detail which helped us confirm cases were indeed nomination violence. For instance, in Bweengwa in Southern province two monitors did not report any nomination violence whereas one monitor described how UPND supporters attacked PF supporters in one incident during nominations. Several vehicles were damaged including the district commissioner's. Given the non-partisan nature of respondents and that interviewers pressed respondents for clarification, we are confident that even if only one respondent in a constituency provided a report of election violence, it did indeed occur. We therefore code *nomination violence* as 1 if just one monitor in a constituency said it occurred.

We opted for a dichotomous coding of the dependent variable. This, however, was not the only available option. We could also have coded a categorical dependent variable to account for variations in severity or a count variable to account for the number of events in a constituency. Nevertheless, we argue that the dichotomous dependent variable is preferable given that there is little variation in both frequency and severity between the constituencies. Only one constituency, Lusaka Central, had more than one reported event. The best way to determine severity would be to utilize reports of injuries, however only three constituencies had such reports (see Table 1).

We do not claim that our data are a perfect reflection of reality. Needless to say, electoral violence is often hard to detect and it is perfectly possible that none of our three monitors picked up on events that occurred during the nomination. To guard against further risk of underestimating nomination violence, we triangulated our reports with the ACLED data.[45] We unearthed two further constituencies with incidents of nomination violence. Our data, all social science data, are imperfect. That the fact that we identified nomination violence in 16 constituencies, compared to only two in ACLED, shows the comparative edge of our approach to data collection.

As *nomination violence* is dichotomous, we use logistical regression models to esti-mate its likelihood. Province-clustered standard errors are used to account for the lack of independence between constituencies within the same province. We use province rather than district-clustered standard errors as some districts contain only one constituency.[46]

Independent variables

Our first hypothesis expects low levels of inter-party competition increase the likelihood of *nomination violence*. For H_1, we operationalize inter-party competition with *2015 competition*, a measure of the constituency's competitiveness based on the 2015 presi-dential by-election. Although our hypothesis concerns the parliamentary elections, as discussed earlier, split-ticket voting is relatively uncommon in Zambia, and the 2015 presidential results at the constituency level are highly correlated with the 2016 parlia-mentary vote shares.[47]

The second hypothesis expects that increased intra-party competition should make *nomination violence* more likely. *Incumbent* captures whether there was a PF or UPND incumbent on the list of candidates considered by each party's NEC for that constitu-ency. The presence of an incumbent should make *nomination violence* less likely.

H_3 expects that where the rules governing the nomination process have been vio-lated, *nomination violence* is more likely. Although it is by no means the only way that intra-party democratic procedures can be violated, we capture this with *imposed candidate*. This is a binary variable coded 1 if the candidate that stood for the PF or UPND was not on the final list of candidates submitted to each party for that constitu-ency. We expect that if either party's NEC imposed a candidate that had not been con-sidered and vetted by the constituency, district, and province, the probability of *nomination violence* increases. The data were obtained directly from the central party offices in Lusaka in the days following the general election. While these data are unique, they have limitations. Ultimately, it would be preferable to have the rankings of the candidates. For each constituency, we can see the list of candidates submitted to each party's NEC, but we have no way of identifying who the constituency's, dis-trict's, or province's preferred choice(s) were. This means that the NEC could still have chosen a candidate that was not ranked first by local branches.

The final hypothesis expects that more rural constituencies have a higher probability of nomination violence. We measure *population density* via number of people per m^2.[48]

We control for a range of demographic, political, and socio-economic characteristics at the constituency level that are likely correlated with the dependent and independent variables. As poorer locations have been shown to be more prone to violence,[49] we include economic development in terms of *night lights (log)*.[50] Satellite night light data have been shown to be an effective proxy for local economic activity.[51] For each consti-tuency we take the mean score, divide it by the land area to get the mean night lights per square kilometre, add 1 to avoid losing observations that equal 0, and take the natural log. We include *literacy*, which is the percentage of literate citizens. We control for ethnic ten-sions as a cause of violence around elections[52] by using the shares of different ethnicity within each constituency to calculate a Herfindahl Index for *ethnic fractionalization*.[53] Higher values of the variable indicate a more ethnically heterogeneous constituency. Finally, we control for the history of violence in the constituency. The data come from ACLED and the SCAD. The categorical variable is coded 0 when no violence was mentioned by ACLED or SCAD in a constituency for elections since the return to multi-partyism, 1 for widely reported violence in one previous election, and 2 for widely reported violence in more than one previous election. The summary statistics including the additional events from ACLED are captured in Table 2.[54]

Results

Table 3 contains the results of the logistical regression models testing the hypotheses. In summary, we do not find support for the inter-party competition hypotheses; the presence of a dominant party is not statistically significant. The indicator capturing whether intra-party democratic rules have been violated is in the expected direction, but this effect is also not statistically significant. However, there is strong support for the notion that a decreased level of intra-party competition diminishes the likelihood of nomination violence, and for the expectation that *nomination violence* is more likely in rural constituencies.

Model 1 tests all hypotheses simultaneously. We expected that the presence of a dominant party would make *nomination violence* more likely. However, the coefficient for *2015 competition* is, unexpectedly, positive although it is not statistically significant. Model 1 does suggest strong support for the intra-party competition hypothesis. We expected that the presence of an incumbent competing for the nomination would make *nomination violence* less likely. *Incumbent* is both negative and highly statistically significant (p-value < 0.01). The hypothesis that imposing a candidate on a constituency would increase *nomination violence* receives limited support. *Imposed candidate* is in the expected direction but it is not statistically significant. Finally, the bargaining power hypothesis receives strong support as *population density* is negative and statistically significant (p-value < 0.01). More rural constituencies make *nomination violence* more likely. The relationship between population density and violence is the complete opposite of what we would expect in the general election campaign.[55] A related study investigates election violence in the Zambian 2016 campaign period and finds that, indeed, here violence is more common in densely populated constituencies.[56] This finding underscores the strong contrast between violence perpetrated during the nomination phase and the general election.

We then test the hypotheses by estimating models with just standard control variables, as per the literature, and the specific independent variables of theoretical interest.

Table 2. Summary statistics.

Variable	Mean	Standard deviation	Minimum	Maximum	Mode
Nomination violence	0.12	0.32	0	1	0
2015 competition	0.28	0.22	0.01	0.96	
Incumbent	0.74	0.44	0	1	1
PF incumbent	0.53	0.50	0	1	1
UPND incumbent	0.21	0.41	0	1	0
Incumbent (years) – log	1.43	0.94	0	2.77	
Imposed candidate	0.26	0.44	0	1	0
Population density	0.00	0.00	0.00	0.01	
Night lights (log)	1.49	2.65	0	11.27	
Violence history	0.18	0.48	0	2	0
Literacy	66.76	12.15	39.81	92.12	
Ethnic fractionalization	0.52	0.25	0.19	0.99	

Table 3. Logistical regression models of the likelihood of *nomination violence*.

	Model 1 All hypotheses	Model 2 H_1	Model 3 H_2	Model 4	Model 5 H_3
2015 competition	1.22	1.31	1.31	1.56*	1.22
	(0.87)	(0.82)	(0.82)	(0.91)	(0.87)
Incumbent	−1.14***	−1.22***	−1.22***		−1.14***
	(0.39)	(0.33)	(0.33)		(0.39)
PF incumbent				−1.73***	
				(0.37)	
UPND incumbent				−0.31	
				(0.85)	
Imposed candidate	0.55				0.55
	(0.50)				(0.50)
Population density	−637.48***	−672.45***	−672.45***	−670.46***	−637.48***
	(200.94)	(228.85)	(228.85)	(206.69)	(200.94)
Night lights (log)	0.17	0.21	0.21	0.27	0.17
	(0.17)	(0.17)	(0.17)	(0.17)	(0.17)
Violence history	−0.25	−0.21	−0.21	−0.28	−0.25
	(0.52)	(0.54)	(0.54)	(0.65)	(0.52)
Literacy	−0.04	−0.05	−0.05	−0.05	−0.04
	(0.05)	(0.05)	(0.05)	(0.05)	(0.05)
Ethnic fractionalization	2.18	2.21	2.21	2.06	2.12
	(1.90)	(1.91)	(1.91)	(1.99)	(1.90)
Constant	−0.16	−0.00	−0.00	0.22	−0.26
	(2.53)	(2.62)	(2.62)	(2.61)	(2.53)
Observations	156				
Pseudo R^2	0.15	0.14	0.14	0.17	0.15

Note: Data come from ZEMS 2016. Robust standard errors clustered by province in parentheses. ***$p < 0.01$, **$p < 0.05$, *$p < 0.10$.

Further, despite their theoretical role in specific hypotheses, we include the indicators of the competitiveness of the constituency and whether there was an incumbent in all models, as previous research has suggested the importance of these factors in explaining election violence.[57] The models would likely feature omitted variable bias without them. The findings are robust across alternative specifications.

Within these models, we conduct an additional test on the intra-party competition hypothesis. Given there is strong support for this hypothesis it makes sense to probe the finding further. In model 4, we disaggregate the effect of whether an incumbent contested the nomination across the PF and UPND. If a PF incumbent contested the nomination, this is expected to decrease the likelihood of *nomination violence* with more than 99% confidence. However, if a UPND incumbent contested the nomination, it is still expected to decrease the likelihood of *nomination violence*, but it is no longer statistically significant. This makes sense theoretically, given that government MPs will have access to more resources than opposition MPs.[58]

We now demonstrate the substantive effects from the two hypotheses for which we found statistically significant support: the intra-party competition, and bargaining power hypotheses. For the former hypothesis, we estimate changes in predicted probabilities of *nomination violence* by altering the value of *incumbent* after estimating models 3 and 4. We hold other independent variables at their average (continuous) or mode (binary). We alter *incumbent*, as well as the disaggregated variables relating to the PF and UPND, from 0 to 1. The results are in Table 4. Ninety-five percent confidence intervals are displayed in brackets, while the bottom half of the table describes the changing values of the variables of theoretical interest.

Table 4. Changes in predicted probability of *nomination violence*.

	Change in predicted probability		
	Model 3	Model 4	
	Incumbent	PF incumbent	UPND incumbent
Pr(y = Nomination Violence)	−0.12	−0.14	−0.01
	[−0.23, −0.08]	[−0.24, −0.04]	[−0.06, 0.04]
		Values of Explanatory Variables	
Low		0	
High		1	

The presence of an incumbent from either party contesting a nomination decreases the likelihood of *nomination violence* by 66%. This is beyond doubt an important and large substantive effect. The effect of just a PF incumbent contesting a nomination decreases the probability of *nomination violence* by 79%. Finally, the effect of a UPND incumbent contesting a nomination decreases the probability of *nomination violence* by only 26%. As per model 4 though, this final estimation is not statistically significant.

We confirm these substantive effects by using the observed values approach to calculate the marginal effects of an incumbent contesting the nomination, as well as the effect of the disaggregated measures, and then average over all the cases.[59] This confirms the findings from the predicted probabilities. The average first differences from changing *incumbent* (−0.13), *PF incumbent* (−0.16), and *UPND incumbent* (−0.03), are very similar to the changes in predicted probabilities outlined in Table 4. The distribution of first differences of changing the variables of theoretical interest for models 3 and 4 is captured in Figure 3. The dashed line in each panel represents the average first difference.

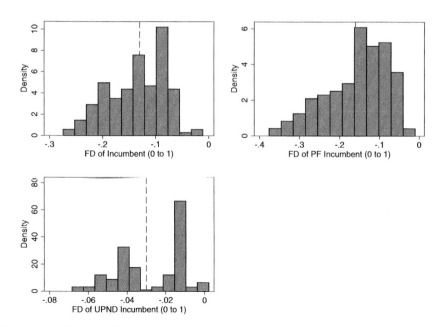

Figure 3. First differences of changing the presence of an incumbent contesting the nomination on the probability of *nomination violence*.

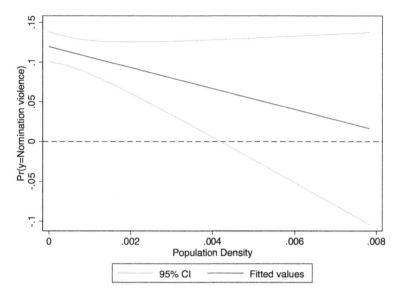

Figure 4. Predicted probability of *nomination violence* based on *population density*.

We now demonstrate the substantive effect of the bargaining power hypothesis. Figure 4 shows the diminishing likelihood of *nomination violence* occurring as constituencies become more rural (after estimating model 1). We have far fewer data points from more densely populated constituencies, which explains the widening of the confidence intervals. This illustrates the statistically significant effect of *population density* decreasing the likelihood of *nomination violence* until *population density* reaches just over 0.004.

Finally, almost none of the control variables we included had a statistically significant effect on the probability of *nomination violence* occurring. This in itself is interesting, given their role in previous studies in helping to explain election violence. Clearly, further work is required to explain nomination violence. Our study represents a first cut: the data strongly support the intra-party competition and bargaining power hypotheses; the intra-party democracy hypothesis should not be discounted; while the data do not support the inter-party competition hypothesis.

Conclusion

Research on election violence is still at an early stage, conceptually, methodologically, and theoretically. Most election violence research has focused on violence during general election campaigns, meaning the literature has been almost silent on the possibility of violence during candidate nominations. This study contributes to the debate on election violence by leveraging a systematic inquiry into subnational variations in nomination violence in the case of Zambia.

We have argued nomination violence can be a manifestation of both vertical and horizontal conflict; in other words, an expression of conflict between local elites and between local and national party elites. An important realization of any theorizing about nomination violation in African contexts is that the weak institutionalization of political parties makes the distinction between intra- and inter-party politics fluid. Local elites flow between parties and the bargaining between central and local elites is an ongoing process. The fluidity of political parties often makes intra-party conflict as likely as inter-party conflict. The results in this explorative study point to the importance of personal candidate resources as an important factor mitigating the risk of nomination conflict. More than low inter-party competition, our analyses show that the presence of an incumbent MP, especially one from the ruling party, reduces the likelihood of nomination violence. We also find that constituencies with low population density are more likely than high population density constituencies to experience nomination violence. This finding is interesting given that general election violence is often associated with urban areas[60] and highlights the often vertical character of nomination conflict between the centre and the periphery.

This study was confined to one country, but had the distinct advantage of introducing systematic data at the constituency level. Election violence research has often suffered from important ecological fallacies when studied from a cross-national perspective. Using national aggregates to study correlates of nomination violence would be especially problematic given the predominantly local character of nomination violence. The method employed in this study could easily be extended to more cases and provide a broader basis for evaluating theories of nomination violence.

This study has implications for research on election violence, but also party politics. The role of coercion and violence in the distribution of power within African parties is still under-theorized. Whereas research on election manipulation more broadly has acknowledged the importance of both violence and bribery as items on the "menu of manipulation",[61] much more emphasis has been put on bribery than violence as an illicit tool to gain power and influence within political parties. Further research should look closer at the possible interchangeability of these two tools.

Notes

1. bbc.com, "South Africa Unrest."
2. Nyasatimes, "Mwalwanda Trounces Mwenifumbo in PP Primaries."
3. Bratton, "Vote Buying"; Collier and Vicente, "Violence, Bribery, and Fraud"; Hafner-Burton, Hyde, and Jablonski, "When Do Governments Resort to Election Violence?"; Fjelde and Höglund, "Electoral Institutions and Electoral Violence in Sub-Saharan Africa."
4. Wahman, "Nationalized Incumbents and Regional Challengers."
5. Goldring and Wahman, "Democracy in Reverse."
6. For example, Fjelde and Höglund, "Electoral Institutions and Electoral Violence in Sub-Saharan Africa"; Taylor, Pevehouse, and Straus, "Perils of Pluralism."
7. Wilkinson, *Votes and Violence.*
8. Seeberg, Wahman, and Skaaning, "Candidate Nomination."
9. Höglund, "Electoral Violence."
10. van de Walle, "Meet the New Boss."
11. Lindberg, "What Accountability Pressures"; Ichino and Nathan, "Primaries on Demand?"
12. Kanyinga, "The Legacy of the White Highlands"; Boone, "Politically Allocated Land Rights"; Straus, "'It's Sheer Horror Here'."
13. Arriola and Johnson, "Electoral Violence in Democratizing States"; Hafner-Burton, Hyde, and Jablonski, "When Governments Resort Resort to Election Violence?"
14. Kjær, "Proxy Wars"; Giollabhuí, "Battleground."
15. Lindberg, "What Accountability Pressures"; Ichino and Nathan, "Primaries on Demand?"
16. Mamdani, *Citizen and Subject.*
17. van de Walle, "Meet the New Boss."

18. Baldwin, "Why Vote with the Chief?"
19. Öhman, "The Heart and Soul of the Party."
20. Norris, *Why Electoral Integrity Matters.*
21. Tucker, "Enough!"; Daxecker, "All Quiet on Election Day?"
22. Weissenbach, "Political Party Assistance in Transition."
23. Straus, "'It's Sheer Horror Here'."
24. Dercon and Guitérrez-Romero, "Triggers and Characteristics."
25. They initially disqualified two candidates, but decided to revoke these disqualifications due to protest. Baylis and Szeftel, "Elections in the One-Party State."
26. Boone, *Political Topographies of the African State.*
27. Levitsky and Way, *Competitive Authoritarianism*; Bogaards and Elicsher, "Democratization and Competitive Authoritarianism in Africa Revisited."
28. Goldring and Wahman, "Democracy in Reverse."
29. Erdmann and Simuntayi, *Transitions in Zambia*; Rakner and Svåsand, "From Dominant to Competitive Party System."
30. Seeberg, Wahman, and Skaaning, "Candidate Nomination."
31. Author interviews Nyambe 07/27/2016 and Phiri 08/04/2016.
32. Ichino and Nathan, "Primaries on Demand?"
33. FODEP, "Press Statement."
34. Rakner and Svåsand, "From Dominant to Competitive Party System," fn 25.
35. Baylis and Szeftel, "Elections in the One-Party State."
36. FODEP, "Press Statement."
37. As described below, via triangulation of our data with ACLED data, we are confident nomination violence occurred in two further constituencies.
38. This was in Lusaka Central where members of the Movement for Multiparty Democracy were throwing stones at their secretariat and damaged vehicles and public busses.
39. Lusakatimes, "Livingstone Nominations Marred with UPND Confusion."
40. We define serious property damage as cases where property of substantial value was totally destroyed. For instance, we would define houses or cars being burned down as serious property damage, whereas a smashed windscreen does not qualify. Consistencies may have had both injuries and serious property damage. Our classifications are made based on narratives left by observers in the surveys.
41. We surveyed three monitors in each constituency except Dundumwezi, Namwala, and Zambezi West. In Dundumwezi, phone signal is non-existent but we managed to interview one observer, while in Namwala and Zambezi West we only managed to speak to two respondents in each constituency.
42. Norris, Frank, and Martínez i Coma, "Measuring Electoral Integrity."
43. Linke, "The Aftermath of Election Crisis"; Ishiyama, Gomez, and Stewart, "Does Conflict Lead to Ethnic Particularism?"
44. Weidmann, "A Closer Look at Reporting Bias in Conflict Data."
45. Raleigh et al., "Introducing ACLED."
46. In the online appendix we conduct a robustness test using district-clustered standard errors and the findings are unchanged.
47. An indicator for the 2015 presidential UPND vote share is correlated with 2016 UPND parliamentary vote share at 0.97, while the equivalent figure for the PF is 0.96.
48. Central Statistical Office, *Zambia.*
49. Collier, *Wars, Guns, and Votes.*
50. Boone, "Spatial Inequalities in African Political Economy Dataset."
51. Henderson, Storeygard, and Weil, "Measuring Economic Growth From Outer Space."
52. Cederman, Gleditsch, and Hug, "Elections and Ethnic Civil War."
53. This has previously been used as a measure of ethnic fractionalization (e.g. Easterly and Levine, "Africa's Growth Tragedy").
54. The data for *literacy* and *ethnic fractionalization* are collected from the 2010 Housing and Population Census and aggregated to the constituency level by the Zambia Central Statistical Office.
55. Dercon and Guitérrez-Romero, "Triggers and Characteristics."
56. von Borzyskowski and Wahman, "The Causes and Consequences."
57. Straus and Taylor, "Democratization and Election Violence."

58. We conduct an additional robustness test, examining the effect of the number of years that an incumbent has served in the National Assembly on the likelihood of *nomination violence*. As one would expect, as the number of years an incumbent has served increases, the likelihood of *nomination violence* decreases.
59. Hanmer and Kalkan, "Behind the Curve."
60. Dercon and Guitiérrez-Romero, "Triggers and Characteristics."
61. Schedler, "The Menu of Manipulation."

Acknowledgements

We are grateful to Chimfwembe Mweenge at the Foundation for Democratic Process (FODEP), Boniface Cheembe at the Southern African Center for the Constructive Resolution of Disputes (SACCORD), and Marja Hinfelaar. Josephine Chanda, Hope Chipalo, Andrew Kasiya, Lwiindi Mweene, Beauty Nalwendo, Beverly Sichilenge, and Prisca Tembo provided outstanding research assistance. We are thankful for comments from the participants at the CODE Workshop at the University of Aarhus, 30–31 March 2017. We are particularly grateful to Merete Bech Seeberg, Anne-Mette Kjær, Svend-Erik Skaaning, and Lars Svåsand. We also like to thank Kostadis Papaioannou for help with processing geographical data and Catherine Boone for data on night light density.

Disclosure statement

No potential conflict of interest was reported by the authors.

Funding

The project has been approved by the Det Frie Forskningsråd; University of Missouri IRB Office #2004569. Funding was provided by the University of Missouri Research Council, Magnus Bergvall's Foundation, and the Danish Innovation Fund.

Bibliography

Arriola, Leonardo, and Chelsea Johnson. "Electoral Violence in Democratizing States." Unpublished Manuscript, University of California, Berkeley, 2012.
Baldwin, Kate. "Why Vote with the Chief? Political Connections and Public Goods Provision in Zambia." *American Journal of Political Science* 57, no. 4 (2013): 794–809.
Baylis, Carolyn, and Morris Szeftel. "Elections in the One-Party State." In *The Dynamics of the One-Party State in Zambia*, edited by Cherry Gertzel, Carolyn Baylies, and Morris Szeftel, 29–57. Manchester: Manchester University Press, 1984.
bbc.com, 06/20/2016. "South Africa Unrest Over ANC's Tshwane Candidate." http://www.bbc.com/news/world-africa-36584572.
Bogaards, Matthijs, and Sebastian Elischer. "Democratization and Competitive Authoritarianism in Africa Revisited." *Zeitschrift für Vergleichende Politikwissenschaft* 10, no. 6 (2016): 5–18.
Boone, Catherine. *Political Topographies of the African State: Territorial Authority and Institutional Choice*. Cambridge: Cambridge University Press, 2003.

Boone, Catherine. "Politically Allocated Land Rights and the Geography of Election Violence: The Case of Kenya in the 1990s." *Comparative Political Studies* 48, no. 2 (2011): 173–202.

Boone, Catherine. 2016. "Spatial Inequalities in African Political Economy Dataset." LSE RIIF 2016 (#1-BRD-B076).

von Borzyskowski, Inken, and Michael Wahman. "The Causes and Consequences of Reporting Bias in Media-based Conflict Event Data." Paper presented at Brown bag Seminar, Uppsala University, Department of Peace and Conflict Studies, March 27, 2017.

Bratton, Michael. "Vote Buying and Violence in Nigerian Elections." *Electoral Studies* 27 (2008): 621–632.

Cederman, Lars-Erik, Kristian Skrede Gleditsch, and Simon Hug. "Elections and Ethnic Civil War." *Comparative Political Studies* 46, no. 3 (2013): 387–417.

Central Statistical Office. *Zambia: 2010 Census of Population and Housing.* Lusaka: Central Statistical Office, 2012.

Collier, Paul. *Wars, Guns, and Votes: Democracy in Dangerous Places.* New York: Harper Collins, 2009.

Collier, Paul, and Pedro C. Vicente. "Violence, Bribery, and Fraud: The Political Economy of Elections in Sub-Saharan Africa." *Public Choice* 153, no. 1–2 (2012): 117–147.

Dercon, Stefan, and Roxana Gutiérrez-Romero. "Triggers and Characteristics of the 2007 Kenyan Election Violence." *World Development* 40, no. 4 (2012): 731–744.

Daxecker, Ursula E. "All Quiet on Election Day? International Election Observation and Incentives for Pre-Electoral Violence in African Elections." *Electoral Studies* 34 (2014): 232–243.

Easterly, William, and Ross Levine. "Africa's Growth Tragedy: Policies and Ethnic Divisions." *The Quarterly Journal of Economics* 112, no. 4 (1997): 1203–1250.

Erdmann, Gero, and Neo Simunatanyi. *Transitions in Zambia: The Hybridisation of the Third Republic.* Lusaka: Konrad Ardenauer Foundation, 2003.

Fjelde, Hanna, and Kristine Höglund. "Electoral Institutions and Electoral Violence in Sub-Saharan Africa." *British Journal of Political Science* 46 (2016): 297–320.

Foundation for Democratic Process (FODEP). "Press Statement on the Just Ended Adoption and Nomination Process." 06/07/2016.

Giollabhuí, Shane Mac. "Battleground: Candidate Selection and Violence in Africa's Dominant Political Parties." This issue.

Goldring, Edward, and Michael Wahman. "Democracy in Reverse: The 2016 General Election in Zambia." *Africa Spectrum* 51, no. 3 (2016): 107–121.

Hafner-Burton, Emilie, Susan D. Hyde, and Ryan Jablonski. "When Do Governments Resort to Election Violence?" *British Journal of Political Science* 44, no. 1 (2014): 149–179.

Hanmer, Michael J., and Kerem Ozan Kalkan. "Behind the Curve: Clarifying the Best Approach to Calculating Predicted Probabilities and Marginal Effects From Limited Dependent Variable Models." *American Journal of Political Science* 57, no. 1 (2013): 263–277.

Henderson, J. V., A. Storeygard, and D. Weil. "Measuring Economic Growth From Outer Space." *American Economic Review* 102, no. 2 (2012): 994–1028.

Höglund, Kristine. "Electoral Violence in Conflict-Ridden Societies: Concepts, Causes, and Consequences." *Terrorism and Political Violence* 21, no. 3 (2009): 412–427.

Ichino, Nahomi, and Noah L. Nathan. "Primaries on Demand? Intra-Party Politics and Nominations in Ghana." *British Journal of Political Science* 42, no. 4 (2012): 769–791.

Ishiyama, John, Amalia Pulido Gomez, and Brandon Stewart. "Does Conflict Lead to Ethnic Particularism? Electoral Violence and Ethnicity in Kenya 2005–2008" *Nationalism and Ethnic Politics* 22 (2016): 300–321.

Kanyinga, Karuti. "The Legacy of the White Highlands: Land Rights, Ethnicity and the Post-2007 Election Violence in Kenya." *Journal of Contemporary African Studies* 27, no. 3 (2009): 325–44.

Kjær, Anne Mette. "'Proxy Wars' in African Dominant Party Primaries: Exploring Triggers of Violence." This issue.

Levitsky, Stephen, and Lucan Way. *Competitive Authoritarianism: Hybrid Regimes After the Cold War.* New York: Cambridge University Press, 2010.

Lindberg, Staffan. "What Accountability Pressures do MPs in Africa Face and How do They Respond? Evidence From Ghana." *The Journal of Modern African Studies* 48, no. 1 (2010): 117–42.

Linke, Andrew. "The Aftermath of Election Crisis: Kenyan Attitudes and Influence of Individual-Level and Locality Violence." *Political Geography* 37 (2013): 5–17.

Lusakatimes.com, 05/31/2016. "Livingstone Nominations Marred with UPND Confusion." https://www.lusakatimes.com/2016/05/31/livingstone-nominations-marred-upnd-confusion/.

Mamdani, Mahmood. *Citizen and Subject: Contemporary Africa and the Legacy of Late Colonialism.* Princeton, NJ: Princeton University Press, 1996.

Norris, Pippa. *Why Electoral Integrity Matters.* Cambridge: Cambridge University Press, 2014.

Norris, Pippa, Richard W. Frank, Ferran Martínez i Coma. "Measuring Electoral Integrity Around the World: A New Dataset." *PS: Political Science & Politics* 47, no. 4 (2014): 789–798.

Nyasatimes, 12/26/2013. "Mwalwanda Trounces Mwenifumbo in PP Primaries: Karonga Central." http://www.nyasatimes.com/2013/12/22/mwalwanda-trounces-mwenifumbo-in-pp-primaries-karonga-central/.

Rakner, Lise, and Lars Svåsand. "From Dominant to Competitive Party System: The Zambian Experience." *Party Politics* 10, no. 1 (2004): 49–68.

Raleigh, Clionadh, Andrew Linke, Håvard Hegre, and Joakim Karlsen. "Introducing ACLED: An Armed Conflict Location and Event Dataset." *Journal of Peace Research* 47, no. 5 (2010): 651–660.

Schedler, Andreas. "The Menu of Manipulation." *Journal of Democracy* 13, no. 2 (2002): 36–50.

Seeberg, Merte, Michael Wahman, and Svend-Erik Skaaning. "Candidate Nomination, Intra-Party Democracy, and Election Violence in Africa." This issue.

Straus, Scott. "'It's Sheer Horror Here' Patterns of Violence During the First Four Months of Côte D'Ivoire's Post-Electoral Crisis." *African Affairs* 110, no. 440 (2011): 481–489.

Straus, Scott, and Charlie Taylor. "Democratization and Election Violence in Sub-Saharan Africa, 1990–2008." In *Voting in Fear: Electoral Violence in Sub-Saharan Africa*, edited by Dorina A. Bekoe, 15–38. Washington, DC: United States Institute of Peace, 2012.

Taylor, Charles Fernandes, Jon C. W. Pevehouse, and Scott Straus. "Perils of Pluralism: Electoral Violence and Incumbency in Sub-Saharan Africa." *Journal of Peace Research* 54, no. 3 (2017): 397–411.

Tucker, Joshua A. "Enough! Electoral Fraud, Collective Action Problems, and Post-Communist Colored Revolutions." *Perspectives on Politics* 5, no. 3 (2007): 535–551.

van de Walle, Nicholas. "Meet the New Boss, Same as the Old Boss: The Evolution of Political Clientelism in Africa." In *Patrons, Clients, and Policies: Patterns of Democratic Accountability and Competition*, edited by Herbert Kitschelt, and Steven I. Wilkinson, 50–67. Cambridge: Cambridge University Press, 2007.

Wahman, Michael. "Nationalized Incumbents and Regional Challengers: Opposition- and Incumbent-Party Nationalization in Africa." *Party Politics* 23, no. 3 (2017): 309–322.

Weidmann, Nils. "A Closer Look at Reporting Bias in Conflict Data." *American Journal of Political Science* 60, no. 1 (2016): 206–218.

Weissenbach, Kristina. "Political Party Assistance in Transition: The German 'Stiftungen' in Sub-Saharan Africa." *Democratization* 17, no. 6 (2010): 1225–1249.

Wilkinson, Steven I. *Votes and Violence: Electoral Competition and Ethnic Riots in India.* Cambridge: Cambridge University Press, 2006.

Öhman, Magnus. "The Heart and Soul of the Party: Candidate Selection in Ghana and Africa." PhD diss., Uppsala University, 2004.

Electoral violence during party primaries in Kenya

Fredrick O. Wanyama and Jørgen Elklit

ABSTRACT
Since the restoration of multi-party democracy in Kenya in 1991, elections have witnessed intra-party violence during the primaries for selecting parliamentary and civic seats candidates. This article addresses the question of why electoral violence occurs during party primaries in Kenya and argues that violence is an outcome of the organization of political parties, which has revolved around personalities identified with ethno-regional interests rather than institutionalism. The upshot has been the absence of party institutionalization to establish structures for recruitment of members and organization of primaries. Such organizational weaknesses have denied parties the capacity to match the intense competition for tickets of ethno-regional dominant parties that guarantees nominees to win seats in their strongholds. Intra-party violence has followed. The article submits that intra-party electoral violence in Kenya is a function of the politics of clientelism and ethnicity, both of which have severely hampered the institutionalization of political parties and their capacity to cope with the stiff competition for the tickets of ethno-regional dominant parties.

The transition from a one-party to a multi-party political system in Kenya in 1991 raised expectations for democratization that hinge on free and fair elections. However, multi-party elections since 1992 have not only been perceived as rigged, but they have also been characterized by violence. Electoral violence often occurred between candidates, members, or supporters within political parties rather than between parties.

This has been particularly evident during party primaries for selecting parliamentary and local authority candidates. The selection of presidential candidates has generally been orderly and non-violent. However, the selection of parliamentary and civic authority candidates conducted through "open voting" is often accompanied by manipulation, intimidation of candidates, rigging, fraud, bribery, chaos and incivility that have descended into intra-party violence. The question addressed therefore is: What drives party members and supporters to resort to intra-party violence to resolve their electoral differences?

Whereas studies on party primaries are gaining popularity in developed democracies, spawning data that are increasingly making comparative studies possible,[1] few such studies exist on Africa to offer reference for the question addressed here. The few studies on party primaries in Africa are largely from Ghana, which has fairly strong political parties with a loyal membership compared to the weak parties that are found in Kenya without a defined membership. In any case, the available studies on the subject address the organization of the primaries,[2] selection system and process of primaries,[3] the demand for, and adoption of, party primaries,[4] and the effect of party primaries on electoral performance,[5] thereby leaving out the question of why electoral violence occurs among party members and supporters during primaries in Africa.

To address this question, we contrast the selection of presidential candidates to the primaries for parliamentary and civic elections in Kenya and suggest that the chaotic and anarchic nominations that erupt into electoral violence are functions of a poor institutionalization of political parties in an ethno-regional party dominant system that often predisposes candidates and supporters to engage in violence. This is particularly the case when nominations are held towards the end of the nomination deadline, yet primaries are the decisive phase of the electoral process.

In the absence of systematic datasets on party primaries in Kenya, the article relies on qualitative data derived from a multitude of sources. The article has four parts. The first sets the argument by outlining the concept of institutionalism and relating it to the organization of political parties in Kenya. The second part illustrates the significance of institutionalism in the conduct of an orderly and peaceful selection of presidential candidates, which is a major contrast to the violence that erupts during parliamentary and civic elections primaries. The third part delves into the conduct of parliamentary and civic elections primaries to demonstrate the poor institutionalization of these primaries and the resultant electoral violence in the 2007, 2013, and 2017 elections. The fourth part is the conclusion.

1. Institutionalism and the organization of political parties in Kenya

Institutions have been defined in two ways: On the one hand, mainly by sociologists, as norms, customs, and practices that initially tend to be taken for granted in informal human relationships but gradually develop into regularized behaviour and conventions that take on a rule-like status in social thought and action.[6] This partly explains why sociologists see institutions everywhere, from handshakes to eating manners and marriages.[7] Indeed, for sociologists, any practice or regular behaviour is an institution.

On the other hand, political scientists and economists have a formal understanding of institutions and define them as routine behaviour and relationships that have identifiable regular structures with rules, regulations, and operational procedures. Institutions then become forms of organization with well-defined organizational patterns, rules, regulations, and procedures that govern the interaction of groups; concrete symbols that these groups inhabit or use; and formal behaviour that may coalesce around all these.[8] These regularized arrangements culminate in some order and stability that make predictability possible in organizations. It is against this background that Easton argued that formal political institutions include the state and related structures such as bureaucracies, political parties, party systems, political actors and agencies, and interest groups.[9]

We adopt this formal institutional perspective in order to assess the extent to which the poor institutionalization of parties in Kenya has contributed to electoral violence during party primaries. As already alluded to, institutionalized political parties are founded on the basis of recognizable principles that underlie their ideologies, policies, and membership. Such parties assume the character of a formal organization by developing structures and operational procedures guided by elaborate rules and regulations to enable them to recruit members and to carry out the functions and obligations required to reach out to the electorate and win elections.[10] The resultant structure and operational procedures enable the parties to develop capacity not just to link up with the grassroots and compete for power by articulating policies for the welfare of society, but also to carry out internal activities. However, political parties in Kenya seem not to resonate with this type of organization.

Following the nature of politics in Kenya that converges around ethnicity and patronage,[11] most of the Kenyan parties have been formed and tend to draw support along ethnic lines. Indeed, ethnicity significantly informed the formation of the first national political parties that led the country to independence in 1960. Whereas the Kenya African National Union (KANU) was formed by leaders from the Kikuyu and Luo communities, leaders from the smaller ethnic communities, who feared the Kikuyu-Luo dominance in KANU, embarked on organizing a coalition of their communities that resulted in the formation of the Kenya African Democratic Union among the Abaluyia, Kalenjin, Maasai, and coastal ethnic groups.[12]

Subsequently, KANU would often be associated with the ethnic group of its chairman. During the Moi era, it was thus thought to be a Kalenjin outfit in contrast to the Kikuyu and Luo party that it was considered at its formation. The post-1992 parties have also been primarily identified with the ethnic communities of their founders, with some communities even changing their support to parties in accordance with the allegiance of their leaders. Given that the country's regions have been identified with particular ethnic groups since the colonial period, one consequence of the ethnic basis is that most parties have become primarily ethno-regional parties.[13]

As observed by Riedl with respect to political systems based on patronage,[14] political parties in Kenya also revolve around personalities. The parties tend to be dominated by their founding leaders, who also double up as (perceived) political heads of their ethnic communities. Party leaders have developed elaborate patronage linkages with their ethnic communities, which has enabled them to control the activities and make the most important decisions of the parties. Thus, as much as some of the parties have constitutions that spell out rules and regulations for governing their activities, they are usually violated at will by the party leaders, who are also their financiers.[15]

With parties revolving around influential personalities, most do not have registered members. They operate on the assumption that all persons in the ethnic community of the leader are their supporters and therefore "members". Consequently, it makes sense to see them as belated versions of Duverger's cadre parties,[16] that is, with no particular interest in or need for members, being primarily electoral support creating vehicles. Very few parties have actually held membership recruitment drives, including KANU that used to recruit members during the one-party era. Thus, though KANU may claim to have members, its register is likely to be outdated and of little or no use.[17]

However, some parties have attempted to register members by issuing membership cards, but this process has been abused by contestants for leadership positions buying the cards, or even printing their own, and then dishing out to any individual to turn up and vote for them during party elections. A person can thus hold membership cards for several parties to which he/she does not belong. Virtually all parties have now shed any pretence of registering members, claiming that people from the ethnic group and region from which the leader comes are members of the party.

Consequently, political parties have difficulties with their operational structures. Most parties have not conducted internal elections to confer leadership democratically. Consequently, they do not have structures of delegates that link grassroots supporters to the national level. The result is that such parties have not organized national conferences to elect officials as provided for in their constitutions. Those that have attempted to do so have ended up holding national conferences consisting of "hired delegates" that do not come from the purported regions and are not even party members. This has quite often been evidenced by conflicting lists of delegates from some regions that differ from the persons arriving from the regions for the conference, only to find the hired delegates having already taken their seats. Such delegates are normally hired by politicians to lock out their competitors from attending the conferences. Thus, the national conference turns out to be a mere showcase of the presumptive leader or wealthy elite.[18]

Nevertheless, parties without registered members still attract a significant following. Such following is usually based on ethnicity, as ethnic communities would be supporting their own kinsman to secure the leadership of the country. Alternatively, the following is based on political patronage as where delegates are paid to attend a party's national conference to vote for the patron. With such support bases, party leaders have ignored the need for party membership and have relied on patronage and ethno-regional mobilization of support to personalize party activities to serve their interests, thereby disconnecting the members and the party elite, particularly between elections.

Such members are usually mobilized during elections to play the cosmetic role of installing contestants through party primaries. This has conditioned party primaries in Kenya to manifest quite differently from what one sees elsewhere. Normally, a party primary is conducted among party members (or their representatives) or voters registered as adhering to the party. In Kenya, primaries are to be understood as (very) open primaries, where all interested voters in a constituency can participate in the selection of a party's parliamentary and civic candidates, subject to what might later happen at the party headquarters. This has turned party primaries into huge, sometimes countrywide, elections that have proved difficult for parties to organize and manage.

The regionalization of Kenyan politics means that primaries are particularly intense in parties and constituencies where the national leader (and presidential candidate) belongs to the dominating ethnic group. The expectation is that the ethnic group will not only vote for their man in the presidential contest, but also to a very considerable degree for his party's candidates for parliamentary and civic seats. Consequently, the competition for the ticket of the dominant party in such constituencies becomes particularly intense, leading in some cases to outright violence, as described below.

Furthermore, many parties depend financially on their leaders. This has rendered most parties, particularly in the opposition, so vulnerable that they cannot enforce rules and regulations that adversely affect the interests of the leaders and financiers, again a parallel to many of the old cadre parties.[19]

Kenyan political parties are generally not founded on ideas and ideals. It is only after the formation of the parties that attempts were made to link them to some ideology, particularly when coining electoral manifestos. The lack of party ideals also explains the frequent defections by politicians from one party to another. To politicians, the suitability of a party is not its ideology, but the opportunities for political career advancement in terms of electoral victory that it offers based on the ethnic and regional support it commands.

Political parties in Kenya do not function as institutions. Constitutions with rules and regulations for conducting the affairs of the parties may exist on paper but are not adhered to. Kenya's low level of party institutionalization has rendered internal party democracy a façade and it has contributed to the low level of party system institutionalization as documented by Riedl in her study of the authoritarian origins of African party systems, where Kenya could also have served as an illustrative case.[20]

2. The institutional basis of the selection of presidential candidates

There has been a major contrast in Kenya between the nomination of presidential candidates and the primaries for parliamentary and civic elections. Whereas the political parties have selected their presidential candidates in an orderly, non-violent manner, the primaries for parliamentary and civic elections have been characterized by chaos, incivility, and violence. We attribute this to the attempt to adhere to institutionalism in the selection of presidential candidates and the institutional failure of political parties during the civic and parliamentary primaries. A review of the methods and process of selecting presidential candidates since 2007 may help to appreciate this point and enhance our understanding of the violence in the civic and parliamentary primaries.

In the 2007 elections, not all members of political parties were involved in the selection of presidential candidates. Whereas the Party of National Unity (PNU) settled on its candidate without any contest, the other two main contending parties, Orange Democratic Movement (ODM) and Orange Democratic Movement Party of Kenya (ODM-Kenya) used conferences to select their presidential candidates despite the disagreements over the election of the parties' delegates.[21]

The two parties embarked on the process by inviting candidates to send their applications to their national election boards upon payment of the nomination fee. Whereas ODM-Kenya cleared Kalonzo Musyoka to compete against Julia Ojiambo for the party's ticket, ODM had five aspirants who were considered influential in their respective provinces: Raila Odinga, the Lang'ata MP, who was battling it out with former Vice President Musalia Mudavadi from Western Province, Eldoret North MP William Ruto from Rift Valley, Gachoka MP Joseph Nyaga from Eastern Province, and Najib Balala of Mvita constituency in Coast Province. The nomination of candidates was followed by a campaign period, during which the candidates launched their visions for the country. Though originating from the same ideological background, the visions of ODM candidates differed with regard to emphasis on issues. Ruto, for instance, paid a lot of attention to security by suggesting the integration of the army in the management of cross-border security, while Odinga emphasized infrastructure development as a key contribution to Kenya's economic rejuvenation. Further differences were made through the manner in which the candidates launched their visions. For instance,

Odinga made a major difference from his competitors by getting the launch of his presidential vision televised live by one of the media houses.[22]

ODM-Kenya and ODM held National Delegates' Conferences (NDC) to nominate their presidential candidates. Though both parties had a formula for the number of delegates from each constituency, the fact that the parties did not have registered members gave aspirants a leeway to handpick delegates from their strongholds. That some candidates enjoyed support from larger geographical areas or more densely populated areas than others initially raised fears that the losers may not accept the outcome and that the events would be marred by violence and a breakup of the parties. Nevertheless, such fears were allayed when both events went on undisturbed.

In ODM-Kenya, Kalonzo Musyoka emerged the winner partly because he organized a better function for launching his vision. Furthermore, Kalonzo's support base in ODM-Kenya was wider than Ojiambo's, who conceded defeat. As a gesture of appreciation, Kalonzo chose Ojiambo as his running mate.

In ODM, Raila scooped the presidential ticket through secret ballot at the NDC, beating all his rivals in their respective provinces except in Western Province, where Mudavadi beat Raila by 303 votes to 128.[23] With a resounding victory for Raila, all the losing aspirants conceded defeat and pledged to support the winner. Perhaps in recognition that Mudavadi had beaten him in his stronghold, Raila picked Mudavadi as his running mate. The peaceful nominations were hailed by many observers, some even imagining that Kenya's intra-party democracy had come of age. They were, however, proved wrong by the parliamentary and civic nominations.

In 2013, the general membership of the parties was also not involved in the selection of presidential candidates, because parties were forming coalitions to present a single candidate in order to improve the chances of winning by carving out ethno-regional voting blocs to support the agreed-on candidates. Subsequently, presidential candidates were selected through negotiations and bargaining. This method of selecting presidential candidates was also made necessary by the Elections Act of 2012 and Political Parties Act of 2011 providing for pre-election coalitions.

The first coalition to appear was Jubilee, a merger between Uhuru Kenyatta's National Alliance (TNA) and William Ruto's United Republican Party (URP). The creation of this coalition was informed by the impending trials of Uhuru and Ruto at the International Criminal Court for crimes against humanity in connection with the 2007/2008 post-electoral violence. The two reframed their charges as a conspiracy by leaders in the then government, civil society organizations, and the international community to impose leaders on Kenyans.[24] This, alongside the peace narrative that purported to unite the Kikuyu and Kalenjin communities that were at the forefront of the violence in Rift Valley, rallied these communities to form and support the Jubilee coalition with Uhuru as presidential candidate and Ruto as his running mate.

The formation of Jubilee prompted other parties to identify their candidates for the election. The urge to get strong candidates to face Jubilee saw virtually all leaders of the key political parties face no nomination challenges. Raila Odinga, thus, faced no challenge in ODM, just as Wycliffe Mudavadi became the candidate of United Democratic Front (UDF), while Kalonzo Musyoka secured the leadership of Wiper Democratic Movement (WDM). Thereafter, these candidates embarked on weaving coalitions that could effectively compete with Jubilee and win the elections. It was in these circumstances that the Coalition for Reforms and Democracy (CORD) emerged with Raila Odinga as its presidential candidate.

The selection of presidential candidates in 2017 was informed by the practice in 2013. As Jubilee had settled on Kenyatta running for a second term with Ruto as his running mate, there were no presidential primaries in the party. This gave the opposition the impetus to start discussions for strengthening their coalitions if they were to make an impact in the elections. Whereas disagreements emerged in CORD over who should be selected as the coalition's flag-bearer, Mudavadi suggested the formation of a super alliance to dislodge Jubilee.

Subsequently, the major opposition parties embarked on negotiations to form a coalition with only one candidate in the presidential elections.[25] Whereas all the parties agreed in principle on the need for an alliance, the bone of contention was the sharing of power, particularly the positions of president and deputy president.

Following lengthy negotiations, the leaders agreed to form the National Super Alliance (NASA) coalition. The coalition settled on Odinga as presidential candidate with Musyoka as running mate. The power-sharing agreement gave Mudavadi the post of premier cabinet secretary under whom there would be two deputy premier cabinet secretaries, reserved for leaders of other coalition partners.[26] With the main coalitions selecting their candidates through negotiations and consensus, there were no presidential election primaries. Again, disagreement and violence were not witnessed in the process.

The selection of presidential candidates has thus tended to be orderly and peaceful, partly because the process has involved a manageable number of people relative to the organizational capacity of the parties. Furthermore, the fact that presidential candidates are selected through bargaining and negotiations that culminate in consensus or agreements suggests that some rules of engagement are established and followed. Indeed, political bargaining and negotiations for selection of presidential candidates are becoming a routine and, therefore, are becoming institutionalized. This has steered the parties clear of the chaos and incivility that have quite often turned the primaries for parliamentary and civic elections violent.

3. Electoral violence in parliamentary and civic elections primaries

The fact that political parties in Kenya tend to be more personal rather than institutional has severely affected their ability to establish regular rules, procedures, and structures for conducting their activities. One of the party activities that has been affected by the poor institutionalization is the organization of party primaries. In the absence of rules, procedures, and structures for conducting primaries, political parties have struggled to make ad hoc arrangements for conducting them. Nevertheless, the clientelist politics that obtain in Kenya, which has turned political parties into ethno-regional organizations, have weakened their institutional functioning. The consequence has been chaotic and anarchic primaries that have quite often descended into violence. A review of the parliamentary and civic elections party primaries since 2007 serves to illustrate this point.

3.1 The 2007 parliamentary and civic primaries

The leading political parties in 2007 embarked on the process of nominating their parliamentary and civic candidates by setting up eligibility criteria for candidates and structures for managing the process. Borrowing from previous experiences, all three leading parties, ODM, PNU, and ODM-Kenya, cobbled together election boards based at party headquarters in Nairobi to administer their primaries. This was followed by drafting requirements that candidates had to meet before being cleared to participate in the primaries. Interestingly, the requirements put more emphasis on payment of non-refundable fees than on party membership and political ideals. In addition to the fees, the candidates were also required to fulfil the legal requirements for candidates in the parliamentary and civic general elections, that is, being a Kenyan citizen and a registered voter.[27]

These criteria in reality meant that any voter could be a candidate. This set the ground for the free-for-all primaries that followed in the three parties and they experienced stiff competition for their tickets, mainly in the strongholds of the respective presidential candidates. The general assumption was that parliamentary aspirants cleared by a presidential candidate's party to contest in a constituency within his stronghold would almost be guaranteed to be elected in the general election. Consequently, PNU, ODM, and ODM-Kenya all attracted a host of parliamentary and civic aspirants in their strongholds to warrant each party holding primaries to select a candidate for each constituency and ward.

Whereas the demand for the tickets of these parties among aspirants was palpable, the need for each party to retain its bloc of followers (who were not necessarily registered members) saw them focus on reducing defections to other parties that could arise out of disagreements over the results of the primaries. This consideration saw these three parties hold their parliamentary and civic primaries simultaneously on 16 November 2007, in order to reduce the defection of losers to other parties. Nevertheless, defections still occurred partly due to dissatisfaction with the manner in which the primaries were conducted.

Those who decamped from PNU and ODM to other parties argued that their decision had been prompted by the undemocratic and unfair management of the nominations in the two parties. Indeed, the parliamentary primaries of these parties were marred by widespread irregularities and violence. Some observers described the nominations as "chaotic" and "a major fiasco".[28] The number of reported malpractices, incivility, and undemocratic tendencies justifies such descriptions.

Some of the parties went into the primaries without even agreeing on the voting method to be used. Affiliate parties to PNU had also not resolved the contentious issue of whether or not to field a single candidate in each constituency. Some of the coalition partners insisted on fielding their own candidates, while others preferred fielding a single candidate for the coalition. Uhuru Kenyatta, for example, declared that KANU would field its own parliamentary and civic candidates countrywide, while NARC-Kenya insisted on PNU fielding a single candidate in each constituency. The Democratic Party, which also decided to field its own candidates, accused NARC-Kenya of being an outfit for sitting MPs who wanted to manipulate the exercise and emerge as sole PNU nominees in their constituencies.[29]

Such disagreements were further compounded by an argument over the voting method to be used, more so in PNU. Whereas some PNU supporters argued for the secret ballot, others preferred queue voting, that is, open voting. Though the ODM national election board settled on secret ballot, it had a certain share of shortcomings that contributed to anarchic and chaotic primaries that sometimes witnessed the outbreak of violence. As none of the parties had registered members, they often resorted to using national identity cards and official Electoral Commission of Kenya (ECK) voters' cards to determine voter eligibility. Voting was, therefore, open to all and it became a public function rather than a party affair. This also made it possible to vote in more than one party's primaries, if one so wished.

The lack of party membership also applied to potential candidates. Besides the political leaders, none of the competing candidates were members of the newly formed coalition parties. As a result, parties did not have proper mechanisms for screening those cleared to contest the nominations. This partly explains the large number of candidates vying for nomination, with a constituency like Chepalungu having 42 candidates for the ODM ticket. Individuals who were members of other political parties were still cleared to contest in the ODM primaries. For example, after James Orengo had been re-elected as SDP Chairman, he participated in the ODM nomination for Ugenya constituency without renouncing his SDP membership.[30]

With every person being an eligible voter and a possible candidate in the absence of strict party membership, and parliamentary as well as civic nominations being carried out simultaneously in all 210 constituencies, logistical and management capacity problems quickly surfaced. One problem was the supply of voting materials. None of the parties had the capacity to produce and distribute voting materials to all constituencies in time. For instance, PNU nominations in Mt Kenya region started late in the afternoon due to the late arrival of voting materials. In Embu District, some stations ended up without ballot papers while in other stations names of aspirants were missing on ballot papers. The ODM nominations suffered the same fate. In Ugenya constituency, for example, chaos erupted, with youths chanting "No Mwanga, No nominations", when the name of a leading contender for the ODM ticket, Steve Mwanga, was found missing from the ballot paper.[31]

In places without properly prepared voting materials, people went on to improvise their own after waiting for hours. For ballot boxes, they used cellotaped plastic waste buckets, food containers, and torn cartons. For ballot papers, the 32-page exercise books used in primary schools were on hand.[32] Where such improvisation was not quickly imagined, the voters waited for hours on end. In Nyando constituency, for example, aspirants were still waiting by 5 pm for ballot papers to be printed.[33] Where voters became impatient to wait for the voting materials, each one occasionally ended up declaring his/her candidate the winner. One of the authors witnessed this at ODM's Matayos polling centre in Busia District, where voters failed to get voting materials and ended up declaring the most preferred candidate the winner. Such declarations would sometimes attract arguments on who actually won and the protagonists would resort to violence. This partly explains why violence erupted in some polling centres.

Political parties also encountered logistical problems in appointing and sending polling officials to the voting centres. For instance, PNU nominations were marred by confusion partly because the party headquarters failed to send presiding officers and clerks to polling centres to conduct the exercise following the withdrawal of the Electoral Commission of Kenya officers from the earlier arrangement to manage the party's primaries. ODM also faced similar challenges. In Eldoret South constituency, ODM nominations were delayed due to parallel lists of presiding and returning officers. In Rangwe constituency, some of the ODM polling officers reached their polling centres very late and when they failed to convince the aspirants to postpone the nominations to the next day, they reportedly took off with the voting materials. This contributed to the outbreak of violence in that constituency.[34]

Some candidates, occasionally in collusion with polling officials, capitalized on logistical problems to hijack ballot papers and use them to rig the elections in their favour. In Eldama Ravine constituency, the former MP, Musa Sirma, had to use his gun to scare away angry ODM supporters, who were baying for his blood after ballot papers were found in his car. Sirma had allegedly diverted the ballot papers and was intending to get them marked in his favour and stuffed in the ballot box. In Kericho town, irate voters burnt more than 5,000 ODM ballot papers being transported in a private car to an unknown destination. In Kieni constituency, a PNU presiding officer was arrested with hundreds of ballot papers that he was allegedly attempting mark in favour of a candidate.[35]

There were also cases where nominations were deliberately disrupted by candidates who found themselves probably losing. For instance, in Nairobi's Kasarani constituency, former MP William Omondi stormed an ODM polling station in Roysambu with over 100 armed youths, grabbed ballot papers and tore them into pieces. In Makadara, at Jericho Social Hall, a group of youths stormed the ODM polling centre, beat up a returning officer and burnt ballot papers. In Gatundu North constituency, supporters of former MP, Patrick Muiruri, grabbed and burnt ballot papers in a PNU nomination booth as they hustled the opponent's supporters. In Kuresoi constituency, irate ODM supporters of the outgoing MP, Moses Cheboi, burnt ballot papers at Olenguruone claiming that the returning officer had been compromised to favour Zakayo Cheruiyot. At the civic level, an ODM aspirant in Sokoni ward in Bahari constituency stormed Kiwandani polling station and roughed up the presiding officer before destroying polling materials and running away with two ballot boxes.[36]

The other malpractice reported in the parliamentary and civic primaries was bribery. Many aspirants went out to buy votes as the last resort for survival in hotly contested nominations. During the PNU nominations in Kirinyaga Central, Matere Keriri's agent was ejected from Thaita polling station for allegedly bribing voters. Bribery allegations were also reported in Tetu constituency where Nobel Peace Prize Laureate Wangare Maathai threatened to withdraw from the PNU nominations as one of the aspirants was dishing out bundles of money to voters at polling stations. In Kimilili constituency, ten PNU aspirants called for nullification of results, citing voter bribery as the main reason.[37] Similar allegations were reported in ODM nominations.

There were also incidents of outright rigging, most of which ended in violence. In Westlands constituency, an ODM aspirant stormed a polling station at Westlands Primary School and confiscated voting materials after word went out that a rival, Fred Gumo, had already been given clearance by ODM officials. The incident resulted in running battles between supporters of the two contestants. In Laikipia East constituency, three PNU aspirants refused to accept the nomination results even before the voting had been concluded, on allegations of glaring irregularities.[38]

In Kisumu Town West constituency, the nomination exercise was disrupted in seven polling stations that were strongholds of one of the female ODM aspirants. Rowdy supporters of a leading male contender dispersed the voters, who were allegedly supporters of the female candidate, and destroyed ballot boxes to ensure that there would be no results from those polling stations. Violence was also seen in the ODM stronghold constituencies such as Ugenya, Kanduyi, Amagoro, Nyakach, Alego-Usonga, Nyando and Mt Elgon, where aspirants disagreed or suspected that electoral malpractices were committed.

In the midst of the ensuing chaotic nominations, some losing aspirants dashed from their constituencies to Nairobi to convince and/or con their party headquarters that they had won the nominations in order to get the clearance certificates before the arrival of the true winners. One such loser was the former Nyakach constituency MP, Peter Odoyo, who was almost lynched by an angry mob when he attempted to present the fraudulently obtained clearance certificate to the returning officer. Such fraudulent manoeuvres were precipitated by party headquarters issuing losers with clearance certificates, only for the genuine winners of the primaries to arrive later to claim the certificates. In the circumstances, some parties issued more than one certificate in a constituency. With several clearance certificates from one party for the same constituency, in the midst of the announcement by ECK that it would accept only the first certificate from a party presented to the returning officer, aspirants embarked on strategizing how to beat each other in presenting their certificates.

The ever-changing lists of nominees at the parties' headquarters that went contrary to the expectations of voters triggered further violence in constituencies and at party headquarters. For instance, in Homa Bay town, residents took to the streets to protest an attempt by the ODM election board to impose outgoing Rangwe MP, Philip Okundi, on the constituents after he lost in the primaries. Meanwhile, the unrest in Siaya District over similar contentions quickly spread from Ugenya where James Orengo was preferred by the ODM headquarters over Steve Mwanga, to neighbouring Gem and Alego-Usonga constituencies. As violence ensued in Muhoroni constituency, two contenders presented nomination results to the ODM election board to prove that each of them had beaten former MP Ayiecho Olweny, but the board proceeded to issue the clearance certificate to Olweny.[39]

Such incidents were not confined to ODM nominations. In PNU, the Kamukunji nomination results were also disputed, forcing the party to hold an arbitration meeting. A scuffle ensued during the meeting, during which Brian Otieno Weke assaulted Simon Ng'ang'a, who had allegedly won the nomination. In KANU, then former Mt Elgon MP John Serut was beaten by rowdy youth when he attempted to raid the party headquarters at Hurlingham in Nairobi to claim his clearance certificate after losing the nomination poll.[40]

After a couple of days of demonstrations in the constituencies over the mismanagement of the primaries, the focus of violence shifted to the party headquarters. At Rainbow House, where the ODM secretariat staff had shifted their operations after protesting aspirants had made Orange House inhospitable, goons shattered all windowpanes, damaged computers, and made away with blank nomination certificates. The armed youth were protesting the issuance of nomination certificates to individuals who had lost in the primaries. The PNU secretariat was also at one time thrown into panic and confusion when a civic nomination loser turned up with a gun and a group of hooligans to demand his clearance certificate.[41]

The above examples demonstrate how the parties' low levels of institutionalization and organizational capacity contributed directly to intra-party violence during the nomination and candidate selection phase of the 2007 general elections.

3.2 The 2013 county assembly, parliamentary, and gubernatorial primaries

In addition to the constituency elected MP, the 2010 Constitution created four other elective seats, namely Member of County Assembly (that was to be elected in each civic ward), the Woman Member of Parliament (elected in each county), Senator (elected in each county), and Governor (also elected in each county). This multiplicity of seats created major challenges for political parties to conduct their primaries. Though the 2011 Elections Act attempted to streamline and regulate the party primaries by giving the Independent Electoral and Boundaries Commission (IEBC) some regulatory powers, the political and personal interests that surrounded the selection of candidates rendered the IEBC unable to enforce its regulations.For instance, parties were required to submit their nomination rules to the IEBC at least six months before the date set for submitting party candidates to the commission, which was estimated to be on or before 18 January 2013. The goal was to enable the commission to review the rules to ensure they would engender free and fair primaries. Parties were also required to submit membership lists at least three months before the primaries. The parties were not only expected to use such membership lists to conduct the primaries, but the commission was also to use them to verify that candidates were actually party members.[42]

Unfortunately, parliament amended the 2011 Elections Act to considerably reduce the timelines within which IEBC was to enforce these regulations. More specifically, the amendments on timelines were meant to allow time for losers in party primaries to defect to other parties or contest the elections as independent candidates. Consequently, the parties never complied with the requirements and IEBC did not have time to do anything about it. As a result, political parties did not use membership lists to conduct their primaries as expected, largely, however, because the parties did not have membership lists. Furthermore, most of the parties, particularly the big ones, held primaries for all seats on the last day set by IEBC in order to prevent losers from defecting to other parties. The result was that parties did not conduct the primaries effectively and fairly. There was also no time to arbitrate on disputes, which significantly led aggrieved parties to resort to violence in an effort to be heard within the limited time.[43]

As was the case in 2007, most of the parties had formed election boards at party headquarters in Nairobi to manage their primaries.[44] These boards established the requirements of candidates for respective seats. These were primarily the nomination fees and compliance with the provisions of the 2012 Elections (Amendment) Act. Since the parties did not have registered members, virtually all parties – like in 2007 – went on to qualify any person registered as a voter in a constituency to be eligible to participate in the primaries either as a candidate or voter. All this made the primaries too huge to manage and opened up the possibility for people to participate in the primaries of more than one party. This again set the ground for the "free-for-all" primaries, especially in the presidential candidates' party strongholds. This was based on the assumption that the parliamentary, gubernatorial, and county assembly representative aspirants nominated by the presidential candidate's party within his stronghold stood a fair chance of winning in their respective elections, that is, the same kind of consideration as prevailed in 2007.[45]

In order to reduce defection of losers from one party to another, parties held their primaries on 17 January 2013, just a day prior to the deadline set by IEBC for parties to submit their nominees. With every person being an eligible voter and the nominations being carried out on the same day in all 290 constituencies for five elective seats, logistical and management problems marred the secret ballot method that virtually all parties were using this time around. The primaries ended with many shortcomings that often resulted in anarchic and chaotic scenes, sometimes including the outbreak of violence.[46] This was also observed at first hand in Homa Bay and Siaya counties, precisely as was the case in 2007.[47]

One of the logistical and management problems was the supply of voting materials, as in 2007, and with the same dire consequences. Again, some candidates capitalized on logistical problems to hijack ballot papers for rigging purposes. For instance, in Homa Bay County there were reports of ballot papers found on the streets marked in favour of one of the Senate candidates. Logistical problems were also manifest in the appointment and sending of polling officials to the voting centres. One can really talk of déjà vu: an inadequate number of ballot papers, candidates' names missing, delayed start of voting, postponement of voting to the next day, no arrangements for safeguarding of ballots cast, and presiding officers not showing up.

In some cases, ballot boxes and returning officers were kidnapped and taken to undesignated places to tally the votes and announce particular candidates as winners as happened in the FORD-Kenya primaries for the Funyula constituency seat in Busia County. The returning officer was commandeered to a remote pub from where he announced one of the candidates as the winner without including vote tallies from a number of polling stations.[48]

Furthermore, results for ODM primaries in many constituencies were never declared. Thus, some people were still waiting to vote, while others were waiting for the results from the ODM election board. In the meantime, the ever-changing lists of preferred nominees that went contrary to the expectations of many voters were being generated at the party's headquarters. The anxiety that resulted from these incidents led to the outbreak of violence in Homa Bay and Siaya counties.[49]

These shambolic primaries occasioned a fallout in ODM, not just between the leadership of the party and losing candidates, but also between the party and the electorate. The latter were particularly interested in making their choice in the primaries of the dominant party in the region because they had learnt from the past that it was the primaries that determined the actual winners in the elections. When they were denied a chance to vote – or their votes were not taken into consideration when the nomination was decided on – many of them resigned from the electoral process, some vowing not to participate in the general elections. This forced Raila Odinga to campaign in his Nyanza stronghold to mend fences with the voters, which he had never done in previous elections. With such chaos, manipulations, rigging, and violence in the primaries, those who failed to secure the tickets of their preferred party defected to minor political parties to revive their political ambitions. Those in ODM decamped to join smaller parties in the CORD coalition just as those in Jubilee looked out for smaller parties supporting the election of Uhuru Kenyatta.

3.3 The 2017 county assembly, parliamentary, and gubernatorial primaries

In the run-up to the 2017 elections, attempts were made to improve on the process of conducting primaries by both the IEBC and political parties. For instance, in January 2017, the IEBC published the Elections Operation Plan for 2017, in which a section was devoted to improving the quality of party primaries by scheduling a timeline for the parties to conduct their nominations. Subsequently, IEBC observed the timelines for carrying out electoral activities and kept on reminding parties to comply with such provisions, though it was sometimes forced to go beyond the stated timelines by court cases that challenged some electoral issues.[50] Some political parties, such as ODM, also started their primaries early and issued a staggered calendar for primaries in different counties to avoid nation-wide nominations on a single day.[51] Jubilee, however, went on to plan for primaries on a single day, though the logistical challenge forced it to reschedule the nominations a couple of weeks later for different counties.[52]

Despite such efforts, the 2017 primaries were as chaotic and shambolic as the previous ones. The perennial problem of the lack of an acceptable membership list disrupted nominations in many parties. For instance, Jubilee had a plan to use a membership register, based on a digital smart card for which a member paid KES 20, for its nominations. However, aspiring wealthy politicians quickly bought all available cards and distributed them to their potential voters, together with money, to beat their opponents. The cards, therefore, ran out before the less wealthy aspirants could access them.[53] Indeed, even individuals who wished to register as party members failed to do so due to the lack of cards. In the circumstances, politicians and their supporters in the Jubilee strongholds rejected the use of smart cards and a register in the nominations, which partly caused the cancellation of the party's primaries that had been scheduled for 21 April 2017.

The cancellation of Jubilee's primaries was not just due to contention on the use of smart cards, but also other logistical challenges that, as usual, affected virtually all parties. The challenges included the lack of a register to determine legitimate members, failure to appoint presiding officers for some polling stations, late arrival of presiding officers, late delivery of election materials, lack of means of transport to ferry election materials and officials, shortage of ballot papers, missing names of some candidates on ballot papers, and defective ballot boxes, some without lids, among others.[54]

Where efforts to resolve the issues were not visible, particularly delays in starting voting, the impatient crowds descended into demonstrations that turned not just chaotic, but also violent. Matters got worse where voting had started and allegations of rigging spread. Voters abandoned the voting queues and joined their candidates in demonstrations that turned violent. Indeed, violence was not just triggered by allegations of rigging, but also by disputed results that were not acceptable to some candidates as was the case in the Jubilee results for Gilgil constituency in Nakuru County.[55]

4. Conclusion

It has been our aim to account for the regularity with which party primaries in Kenya have been characterized by chaos, fraud, bribery, and incivility that has quite often descended into intra-party electoral violence. With reference to party primaries for the general elections 2007–2017, we have shown that the organization of political parties in Kenya has not just been driven by ethnicity, but it has revolved around personalities identified with ethno-regional interests. This has given way to the supply of ethno-regional dominant parties in each election, with limited chances for institutionalization. Though some of them have written constitutions, and rules and regulations for conducting their activities, the politics of patronage have rarely allowed parties to adhere to them.

Consequently, parties do not have registered members to whom leaders are accountable; individuals occupy party leadership positions without being elected; founding leaders of political parties dominate their affairs; and the poor resource base of political parties has severely dented their capacity to conduct ordinary party activities. Due to the lack of ideological orientation, ideals, and principles in the political parties, there are frequent defections from one party to another. Indeed, political parties are formed and used as instruments for individual rides to power. Consequently, political parties in Kenya do not function as institutions and one can even suspect that the weak institutionalization is acceptable – at least in some cases – as a means to protect individuals' political interests.

Such weaknesses have hampered the capacity of parties to handle the intense competition for the tickets of ethno-regional dominant parties, where the nomination of a candidate by the dominant party translates into a seat grab. With most political parties involving all members in the nomination of candidates using weak structured selection procedures, in the midst of limited time to organize massive primaries, and a leadership that is reluctant to follow rules and procedures, members have quite often resorted to bribery, manipulations, incivility, and rigging that have particularly marred the parliamentary and civic primaries of the leading political parties. In the absence of appropriate party structures to arbitrate the resultant disputes, both candidates' and members' frustrations have culminated in intra-party electoral violence.

Thus, intra-party electoral violence in Kenya is a function of the politics of clientelism and ethnicity, both of which have severely hampered the institutionalization of political parties and their ability to improve their capacity to cope with the stiff competition for the tickets of ethno-regional dominant parties.

Notes

1. Sandri, Seddone, and Venturino, *Party Primaries.*
2. Wanyama, "Voting without Institutionalized Political Parties."
3. Ohman, "The Heart and Soul."
4. Ichino and Nathan, "Primaries in Demand?"
5. Ichino and Nathan, "Do Primaries Improve Electoral Performance?"
6. Sangmpam, "Politics Rules."
7. Kenny, "Gender, Institutions and Power."
8. Sangmpam, "Politics Rules."
9. Easton, *The Analysis.*
10. Wanjohi, *Political Parties in Kenya*; Wanjohi, "Sustainability of Political Parties."
11. For an extensive discussion of the politics of ethnicity and patronage in Kenya, see Barkan, "Legislators, Elections, and Political Linkage"; Barkan, "Divergence and Convergence"; Oyugi, "Uneasy Alliance"; Oyugi, "Ethnic Politics in Kenya"; Bratton and Kimenyi, "Voting in Kenya," among others.
12. Wanyama, "Voting without Institutionalized Political Parties."
13. Oloo, "The Contemporary Opposition."
14. Riedl, *Authoritarian Origins.*
15. Oloo, "The Contemporary Opposition."
16. Duverger, *Political Parties.*
17. Wanyama, "Voting without Institutionalized Political Parties."
18. Oloo, "The Contemporary Opposition."
19. Ibid.
20. Riedl, *Authoritarian Origins*, 37–42.
21. Wanyama, "Voting without Institutionalized Political Parties."
22. Ibid.
23. *The People Daily*, 2 September 2007.
24. European Union Election Observation, 2013.
25. *The Standard*, 23 February 2017, "NASA Launches Joint Onslaught on Uhuru in August Elections."
26. *Daily Nation*, 28 April 2017, "How NASA Leaders Broke Deadlock on Flag-bearer Choice."
27. *Sunday Standard*, 11 November 2007, "Party Sets Nomination Guidelines."
28. *Saturday Standard*, 17 November 2007, "Party Nomination End in Fiasco."

29. *Daily Nation*, 7 October 2007, "Which Nomination Route for the Party of National Unity?"
30. *Daily Nation*, 30 September 2007, "ODM Nominations Attract Big Numbers."
31. *Saturday Nation*, 17 November 2007.
32. *Saturday Standard*, 17 November 2007, "Party Nomination End in Fiasco."
33. *Saturday Nation*, 17 November 2007, "Confusion and Violence Mar Party Nominations."
34. Ibid.
35. Ibid.
36. *Saturday Standard*, 17 November 2007, "Party Nomination End in Fiasco"; *Saturday Nation*, 17 November 2007, "Confusion and Violence Mar Party Nominations."
37. *Saturday Standard*, 17 November 2007, "Aspirant Steals Papers"; *Sunday Nation*, 18 November 2007, "Kabogo Moves Out of PNU Citing Irregularities."
38. *Sunday Nation*, 18 November 2007, "Kabogo Moves out of PNU Citing Irregularities."
39. *East African Standard*, 20 November 2007, "Turmoil: Guns, Blood and Tears."
40. Ibid; *East African Standard*, 20 November 2007, "Aspirant is Charged with Beating Rival."
41. *East African Standard*, 20 November 2007, "Turmoil: Guns, Blood and Tears."
42. ELOG, *The Historic Vote*.
43. Carter Center, *Observing Kenya's National Elections*, 32–35.
44. Wanyama et al., "Ethnicity and/or Issues?"
45. Ibid.
46. Office of the AU Panel of Eminent African Personalities, *Back from the Brink*, 220.
47. Ibid.
48. Wanyama et al., "Ethnicity and/or Issues?"
49. Office of the AU Panel of Eminent African Personalities, *Back from the Brink*, 220.
50. *Daily Nation*, 10 May 2017, "IEBC Extends Deadline for Nominated Candidates."
51. *Daily Nation*, 16 March 2017, "ODM Pushes Start Date for Nominations by a Week."
52. *Daily Nation*, 21 April 2017, "Jubilee Cancels Primaries in all Counties"; *Daily Nation*, 24 April 2017, "Jubilee Party Reschedules Nominations in 16 Counties."
53. *Daily Nation*, 20 March 2017, "Jubilee under Pressure to Abandon Smart Cards in Primaries."
54. *The Star*, 13 April 2017, "Chaos Marks the First Day of ODM Primaries in Bungoma, Busia"; *Saturday Standard*, 22 April 2017, "Chaos as Key Jubilee Aspirants Boycott Party Nominations Citing Massive Irregularities"; *Daily Nation*, 21 April 2017, "Chaos, Confusion, Anger Hit Jubilee Nominations"; *The East African*, 20 April 2017, "Chaotic, Violent Primaries in Kenya Ominous."
55. *Daily Nation*, 21 April 2017, "Chaos, Confusion, Anger Hit Jubilee Nominations"; *The Star*, 28 April 2017, "Chaos in Gilgil after Jubilee Rival Groups Clash Over Disputed Results."

Acknowledgements

We appreciate very much comments and suggestions from the journal's reviewers and from participants at the March 2017 CODE seminar at Aarhus University on electoral violence.

Disclosure statement

No potential conflict of interest was reported by the authors.

Bibliography

Barkan, Joel D. "Divergence and Convergence in Kenya and Tanzania: Pressures for Reform." In *Beyond Capitalism vs Socialism in Kenya and Tanzania*, edited by Joel D. Barkan, 1–46. Nairobi: East African Educational Publishers, 1994.

Barkan, Joel D. "Legislators, Elections, and Political Linkage." In *Politics and Public Policy in Kenya and Tanzania*, edited by Joel D. Barkan, 72–98. Nairobi: Heinemann, 1984.

Bratton, M., and M. Kimenyi. "Voting in Kenya: Putting Ethnicity in Perspective." *Journal of Eastern African Studies* 2, no. 2 (2008): 272–289.

Carter Center. *Observing Kenya's March 2013 National Elections*. Atlanta, GA: The Carter Center, 2013.

Duverger, Maurice. *Political Parties*. London: Wiley, 1954.

Easton, David. *The Analysis of Political Structure*. New York: Routledge, 1990.

ELOG. *The Historic Vote: Elections 2013*. Nairobi: Elections Observer Group, 2013.

European Union Election Observation Mission to Kenya. General Elections 2013 Final Report, 2013.

Ichino, Nahomi, and Noah L. Nathan. "Do Primaries Improve Electoral Performance? Clientelism and Intra-Party Conflict in Ghana." *American Journal of Political Science* 57, no. 2 (2013): 428–441.

Ichino, Nahomi, and Noah L. Nathan. "Primaries on Demand? Intra-Party Politics and Nominations in Ghana." *British Journal of Political Science* 42 (2012): 769–791.

Kenny, Meryl. "Gender, Institutions and Power: A Critical Review." *Politics* 27, no. 2 (2007): 91–100.

Office of the AU Panel of Eminent African Personalities. *Back from the Brink: The 2008 Mediation Process and Reforms in Kenya*. Addis Ababa: The African Union, 2014.

Ohman, M. "The Heart and Soul of the Party: Candidate Selection in Ghana and Africa." PhD diss., Uppsala University, Sweden, 2004.

Oloo, Adams G. R. "The Contemporary Opposition in Kenya: Between Internal Traits and State Manipulation." In *Kenya: The Struggle for Democracy*, edited by Godwin R. Murunga and Shadrack W. Nasong'o, 90–128. London: Zed Books, 2007.

Oyugi, Walter O. "Ethnic Politics in Kenya." In *Ethnic Conflict in Africa*, edited by Okwudiba Nnoli, 287–309. Dakar: CODESRIA, 1993.

Oyugi, Walter O. "Uneasy Alliance: Party-State Relations in Kenya." In *Politics and Administration in East Africa*, edited by Walter O. Oyugi, 153–192. Nairobi and Bonn: Konrad Adenauer Foundation, 1992.

Riedl, Rachel Beatty. *Authoritarian Origins of Democratic Party Systems in Africa*. New York: Cambridge University Press, 2014.

Sandri, G., A. Seddone, and F. Venturino, eds. *Party Primaries in Comparative Perspective*. London: Routledge, 2016.

Sangmpam, S. N. "Politics Rules: The False Primacy of Institutions in Developing Countries." *Political Studies* 55 (2007): 201–224.

Wanjohi, Nick G. *Political Parties in Kenya: Formation, Policies and Manifestos*. Nairobi: Views Media, 1997.

Wanjohi, Nick G. "Sustainability of Political Parties in Kenya'." In *African Political Parties: Evolution, Institutionalisation and Governance*, edited by M. A. Salih, 239–255. London: Pluto Press, 2003.

Wanyama, Fredrick O. "Voting Without Institutionalized Political Parties: Primaries, Manifestos and the 2007 General Elections in Kenya." In *Tensions and Reversals in Democratic Transitions: The Kenya 2007 General Elections*, edited by K. Kanyinga and D. Okello, 61–100. Nairobi: Society for International Development & Institute for Development Studies, University of Nairobi, 2010.

Wanyama, Fredrick O., Jørgen Elklit, Bodil F. Frederiksen, and Preben Kaarsholm. "Ethnicity and/or Issues? The 2013 General Elections in Western Kenya." *Journal of African Elections* 13, no. 2 (2014): 169–195.

Fighting your friends? A study of intra-party violence in sub-Saharan Africa

Bryce W. Reeder and Merete Bech Seeberg

ABSTRACT
This article focuses on a less visible and less studied type of political violence, namely violence that occurs within political parties. We use new, district-level data to compare the temporal and spatial dynamics of intra-party violence to those of general election violence across selected sub-Saharan African countries, including both democracies and autocracies, from 1998 to 2016. Relying on cross-national and sub-national analyses, we show that intra-party violence follows a unique pattern. First, unlike general election violence, intra-party violence peaks prior to election day as it is often sparked by individual parties' candidate nomination processes. Second, low levels of competitiveness – typically theorized to reduce the risk of election violence – increase the risk of intra-party violence on the sub-national level. Thus, dominant party elections do not necessarily see less election-related violence than hotly contested elections. Rather, violence may be pushed from election day to intra-party competitions. If we neglect the study of violence within political parties, we thus risk underestimating the threat of election violence and misdiagnosing its causes.

An important threat to processes of democratization across the globe is the spread of political violence and more specifically election violence. Political violence is not isolated to dictatorships. In fact, the very processes of democratization and the introduction of elections may increase the risk of violence.[1] A new literature on election violence is busy untangling the causes and consequences of these dynamics. However, it is also increasingly clear that the very visible types of violence with which this literature engages – the regime's oppression of voters and opposition and clashes between supporters of different parties – are far from the only types of election violence. In many regimes, violence plays out not only between parties but also within those parties that were supposed to help develop a peaceful, democratic environment.

The existing literature on election violence neglects intra-party violence. As we argue in this article, intra-party violence tends to occur prior to elections – and often even prior to the campaign – and is thus outside of the temporal scope of many studies of election violence.[2] Furthermore, many existing studies focus on violence carried out

Supplemental data for this article can be accessed at https://doi.org/10.1080/13510347.2018.1441291

by incumbents against voters or opposition[3] or on electoral protests[4] and thus disregard intra-party violence. Others look at election violence in general and do not distinguish between different types of election violence based on perpetrators and victims.[5] They thus risk treating instances of intra-party violence as episodes of general election violence and are unable to identify the unique dynamics of intra-party violence. Finally, the few existing studies of intra-party violence tend to focus on single cases.[6]

Is intra-party violence just another form of general electoral violence following largely identical patterns? In this study, we investigate the timing of intra-party violence across five sub-Saharan African countries and explore the relationship between competitiveness and violence on the sub-national level in two of those cases. We argue that intra-party violence follows a different logic than general election violence. First, as intra-party competition intensifies when parties select candidates to run in elections, intra-party violence tends to occur prior to election day rather than during and after elections. Second, the literature has found that the competitiveness of elections increases the risk of general election violence.[7] However, as the stakes of intra-party competition for nomination are higher if the party's candidates have a greater chance of winning a seat in the upcoming elections, districts with less inter-party competition are more likely to see intra-party violence.

To investigate these questions, we develop a unique dataset of violent events occurring between supporters, members or candidates of the same political party in five sub-Saharan African countries (Ghana, Kenya, South Africa, Uganda, and Zimbabwe) from 1998 to 2016. In addition, we code instances of general election violence that take the form of violence between political parties, government crackdowns on voters, or election-related protests and riots. We analyse the timing of election violence and intra-party violence across all five cases. As levels of competitiveness in elections differ not only across countries and elections but also across constituencies within the same country, we test our hypothesis on competitiveness and violence on the constituency level in Kenya and Zimbabwe. Our analyses reveal several notable patterns across time and space.

First, unlike general election violence, intra-party violence primarily takes place prior to elections when individual parties nominate candidates for inter-party contest. Second, whereas election violence is commonly argued to increase with levels of competitiveness in elections,[8] intra-party violence actually decreases in more competitive districts but increases as inter-party competitiveness declines. Thus, in systems with low inter-party competitiveness (for example, dominant party systems), general election violence may be less common, but levels of violence within political parties increase. Furthermore, this increase in intra-party violence in less competitive districts is strongest in the months prior to elections where we expect intra-party violence to be most frequent.

The findings indicate that by overlooking the unique dynamics of intra-party violence, we disregard a serious threat to the peaceful development and deepening of democracy. Violence within political parties is common: In some of the countries in our sample, intra-party violence made up one-fifth or more of all election violence. Intra-party violence is temporally distinct from general election violence and its drivers are different. Consequently, if we limit the study of election violence to the campaign and post-election period or to inter-party violence, we are likely to underestimate the problems of violence in African political competition and make inaccurate inferences about the factors conducive to electoral violence. To understand and potentially mitigate the threat of election violence, we must look beyond the narrow election period and into the dynamics of the political parties that contest the elections.

This article represents one of the first attempts to do so across several countries. Below, we outline the expected dynamics of intra-party violence and propose two testable empirical predictions. We then describe the data we collected and discuss some general trends. This is followed by a more rigorous analysis of the data and a discussion of the implications of the findings for emerging democracies, as well as scholars of political violence and democratization.

Intra-party violence and its causes

We follow Seeberg, Wahman, and Skaaning's (this issue) definition of nomination violence but extend our focus to all types of intra-party violence – also those that are unrelated to nomination processes – and define intra-party violence as acts or threats of physical harm by supporters, members, or candidates of a political party against supporters, members, or candidates of that same political party (or against their property).

Why do we see violence between supporters and candidates of the same political party, and how does the logic of intra-party violence differ from that of general election violence (that is, inter-party violence)? In the literature on election violence, two characteristics of the election are commonly assumed to affect the risk of violence: the *stakes* of the competition and the level of *competitiveness*.[9]

How do these arguments apply to the logic of intra-party violence? The argument regarding the *stakes* of elections is two-fold. First, not only do the stakes vary across elections – the very nature of elections increases the stakes of political competition as they clearly and visibly pit contenders against each other in a battle for political power.[10] Thus, elections risk becoming focal points for violent conflicts[11] and are generally expected to increase levels of political violence.[12] This unfortunate dynamic of elections is thought to be particularly pertinent in sub-Saharan Africa where neo-patrimonialism is widespread and political institutions are often weak.[13]

The high stakes of national elections also affect intra-party dynamics. Before every national election, individual parties must agree on which candidates to field for the election. We expect this selection process to increase the risk of intra-party violence so that levels of violence are higher during than outside nomination processes. More precisely, we expect to see intra-party violence both prior to a party's nomination process (as an attempt to rig the nomination) as well as after nomination day (as a response to the results of the nomination). This logic does not differ from that of inter-party violence, which is expected to increase during and immediately following the inter-party electoral race. However, as the timing of candidate nominations differs from that of general elections – individual parties' candidate selections typically take place a few months prior to actual elections – the temporal dynamics of intra-party violence and general election violence will differ:

> H1: Whereas inter-party violence primarily occurs during the election campaign and in the weeks immediately following elections, intra-party violence peaks prior to elections.

Intra-party violence may also be unrelated to the actual timing of elections, for instance, when succession struggles occur within authoritarian ruling parties and party elites battle to take over after a leader's sudden death or an ailing leader seeks to establish an heir. Thus, we do not expect intra-party violence to occur only prior to elections, but we do expect it to increase during candidate nomination processes.

Second, just like the mere holding of elections increases the stakes of political competition and thus the risk of both general election violence and intra-party violence, the stakes may also vary across elections. However, we do not expect these dynamics to differ between inter- and intra-party violence. Where the elected position allows the candidate control over ample resources, this is likely to increase the risk of violence both during candidate selection processes and in the actual election. Thus, we do not test the effect of differing stakes of elections on the risk of intra-party violence versus the risk of general election violence.

Competitiveness, the other factor expected to affect the risk of election violence, may have differing effects on inter- and intra-party violence. The existing literature on election violence generally expects high levels of competitiveness to increase the risk of violence.[14] The argument is that using violence to win elections is a costly strategy domestically and internationally. Governments have been shown to employ violence against opposition parties and voters primarily when their rule is threatened, that is, when competitiveness is high.[15] This claim is challenged by Collier and Vicente,[16] who formalize a model in which primarily weak candidates use violence as a tool for electoral manipulation.

We argue that rather than reducing levels of election violence, low competitiveness – or, in other words, party dominance – shifts the stakes of the race, and thus the risk of violence, from inter-party to intra-party competition. If the dominant party's candidate is highly likely to win the electoral race for president or parliamentarian for a certain district, the potential gains of nomination for the candidate and her supporters are higher and so are the incentives to engage in violence. Where inter-party competitiveness is low, violence may occur during the candidate selection process within the dominant party rather than on election day, where the results are already known. Thus, party dominance may change the ratio of intra-party to inter-party violence. The result is not less election violence but a shift from inter-party violence, that is, general election violence, to intra-party violence:

H2: Inter-party competitiveness increases inter-party violence and reduces intra-party violence.

This dynamic is expected to play out on the local rather than on the national level. Party dominance or competitiveness varies both across and within countries. Wahman has recently shown that party nationalization in Africa is generally lower than on other continents – particularly for opposition parties – and most African parties receive a large share of their electoral support in certain regions or districts.[17] The issue is exacerbated in cases where electoral boundaries were drawn to match the ethnic composition of the area.[18] Thus, in many African states, sub-national contests are essentially uncompetitive despite competition between parties on the national level, as was the case for the Kenyan elections of 2013.[19] Relying on state-level measures of electoral competitiveness or party dominance and violence risks obscuring the relationship between intra-party violence and competitiveness. In the empirical analyses, we therefore assess the effect of competitiveness on intra-party violence on the sub-national level.

Furthermore, the hypothesis implies that levels of intra-party violence should differ between parties. If low levels of competitiveness in the general election (either at the national or district level) push the actual competition, and thus the risk of violence, to the candidate nomination process of the (nationally or locally) dominant party, intra-party violence should be concentrated in the party that is expected to win elections. However, as party dominance can vary across districts in the same party system, intra-party violence should not be restricted to incumbent parties. Locally dominant opposition parties would also experience increased risks of violence. We do not distinguish between incumbent and opposition parties in our analysis, but our expectation is in line with Seeberg, Wahman, and Skaaning (in this issue), who find – based on an expert survey – that intra-party violence occurs in both incumbent and opposition parties but is most common in nationally dominant incumbent parties.

Naturally, other factors known to increase the risk of general election violence likely also increase the risk of intra-party violence. The stakes may be higher in presidential than in parliamentary contexts,[20] in majoritarian electoral systems,[21] and where elections give the winner control over natural resources wealth. The rule of law and an efficient and unbiased police and military force that will crack down on perpetrators of violence will increase the costs of engaging in violence and thus lower the incentives for both inter- and intra-party violence.[22] Further, a country coming out of a civil war is probably more vulnerable to outbreaks of both types of violence.[23] As these factors likely affect both intra- and inter-party violence, whereas we expect inter-party competitiveness to explain why some systems see much higher rates of intra-party than inter-party violence, and the factors further show little variation across constituencies, our sub-national analyses focus on the relationship between competitiveness and violence.

Finally, violence is not equally costly across regime types but likely evokes more condemnation in democracies than in autocracies. We thus expect less violence – of either type – in democracies even though competitiveness is higher in democratic regimes. However, hypothesis 2 applies across regime types as we also expect higher levels of intra-party violence in dominant party democracies than in non-dominant party democracies. In the following section, we present our data before proceeding to test our hypotheses.

Data on intra-party violence

What do we know about the propensity of intra-party violence during candidate selection? A number of studies have explored the spread of electoral violence across countries and over time in Africa and globally[24] but none have looked systematically at intra-party violence. Various types of data on elections and violence have emerged, including datasets on acts of violence in general, such as ACLED[25] and the UCDP Georeferenced Event Dataset,[26] datasets recording acts of election-related violence, namely SCAD[27] and AEVD,[28] and datasets recording whether an election was violent, including NELDA,[29] V-Dem,[30] and PEI.[31]

Some of the existing data sources on violence allow us to distinguish between different types of violence, such as riots, civilian killings, and battles (ACLED) or protests, riots, strikes, inter-communal conflict, government violence against civilians, and other forms of social conflict (SCAD). However, there is no dataset that codes whether acts of violence occurred between factions of the same party or had links to processes of candidate selection prior to the actual election campaign.

To acquire such data, we have recoded the recorded violent events in the ACLED dataset to identify *intra-party violence* occurring inside a political party and *general election violence* in the form of inter-party violence, government crackdown on voters or protesters, or election-related protests and riots. We have done so for five sub-Saharan African countries: Uganda, Zimbabwe, South Africa, Ghana, and Kenya. The cases were selected to achieve variation on two main dimensions discussed in the theoretical section: regime type and electoral competitiveness at both the state and district-level. Table 1 illustrates the distribution of cases with regard to national-level variation.

Uganda and Zimbabwe are both autocracies. The National Resistance Movement (NRA) in Uganda is a clearly dominant party that wins a majority of all electoral districts. In Zimbabwe, the Zimbabwe National Union-Patriotic Front (ZANU-PF) is also known to be the electoral winner even before elections have taken place, but unlike in Uganda, many districts are heavily contested, and the opposition continues to win seats particularly in the urban areas.[32] Zimbabwe has low levels of competitiveness on the national level (See Table 1) but not necessarily on the sub-national level.

South Africa, Ghana, and Kenya are all democracies. In South Africa, the African National Congress (ANC) is the dominant party and has been so since the transition to democracy in 1994, whereas the national level of competitiveness in elections is high in Ghana and Kenya. In Ghana, electoral competition is mainly between the two major parties, the National Democratic Congress (NDC) and the New Patriotic Party (NPP), whereas Kenya has a multitude of parties. In both Ghana and Kenya, however, many districts have locally dominant parties even though no parties dominate the entire country. Levels of competitiveness thus vary on the sub-national level in these two countries (not illustrated in Table 1).

The fourth cell is empty as autocracies per definition have low levels of electoral competitiveness on the national level where the ruling party always wins. The selection of cases thus provides variation on the dimensions of national competitiveness in elections and regime type. Furthermore, as levels of electoral competitiveness also vary subnationally, we shift our focus to the constituency level in some analyses, which provides additional variation over time and across constituencies within selected countries.

To determine which events constitute which form of electoral violence, we first scraped the ACLED data for the names of political parties that were involved in the most recent election and several important keywords, such as *election* and *nomination*.[33] We then used human coders to comb through the data and drop events that were unrelated to a recent or forthcoming election and to determine which events constitute which form of violence. Classifying an event as inter- or intra-party violence requires an explicit account of infighting among members of the same party or violence across political parties.[34] Vague events in which actor names or notes attached to an event did not indicate such dynamics were dropped. However, cases with a clear description of popular riots and/or protests related to elections were coded as such and combined with our inter-party violence measure to form our general election violence category.[35] As the ACLED events are geo-coded, we can match violent events to electoral districts and use the measure in our sub-national analyses.

We recognize that ACLED is not the only source from which to derive data on intra-party violence during election periods. In our view, however, it is currently the most

Table 1. Case selection.

	Democracy	Autocracy
High competitiveness	Ghana Kenya	–
Low competitiveness	South Africa	Uganda Zimbabwe

promising source of such data for three reasons. First, unlike the UCDP Georeferenced Data Project, it records violent events involving actors that are not currently engaged in a civil conflict, that is, actions taken by and against political parties, and not only actions by those groups that are actively involved in a campaign against government forces. Second, it registers non-lethal events, which constitute the majority of the incidences of intra-party violence and general election violence that we record. Using the UCDP data, we would lose the majority of all the violent events included in our analysis. Third, the coverage of ACLED relative to other political event data sources, such as SCAD, is notable. Comparisons of ACLED to other sources of data reveal not only more events but also a much more diverse set of events.[36]

Intra-party violence across time and space

In Figure 1(a)–(e), we plot levels of general election violence (red lines) and levels of intra-party violence (blue lines) for the five countries under investigation. The dotted

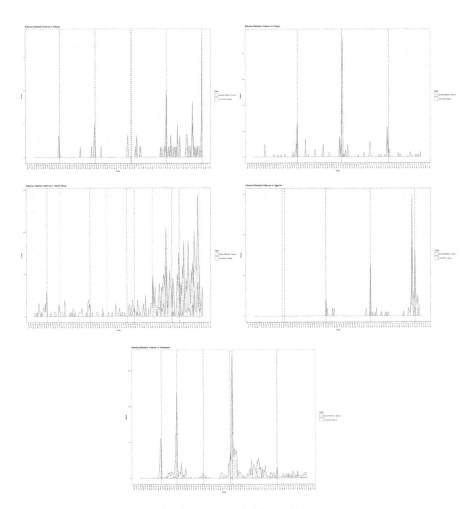

Figure 1. Patterns of violence by political parties in 5 sub-Saharran African countries.

lines indicate elections, and blue dotted lines mark local elections if these were held separately from national level elections. The absolute number of violent events in each country is provided in Table 2. This descriptive analysis hints at both a temporal and a spatial pattern in the distribution of intra-party violence relative to other types of election-related violence.

The figures reveal that both intra-party violence and general election violence tend to spike before election time. General election violence occurs immediately prior to elections, during the actual election and in the electoral aftermath; intra-party violence typically tops a little earlier. In Kenya, where election violence was particularly high in the 2007 elections, levels of general election violence are indeed high. More than 45 instances of election violence are recorded in the period around the 2007 elections (Figure 1(b)), and 159 events are registered throughout the period (Table 2). Intra-party violence is far less common (18 events recorded) but still occurred in each of the three investigated elections. In fact, in the 2013 elections, which were deemed surprisingly peaceful following the tragic and deadly 2007 elections,[37] levels of intra-party violence prior to the election were almost as high as the levels of inter-party violence during the electoral campaign (Figure 1(b)). Furthermore, intra-party violence has a clear temporal dynamic in Kenya: unlike general election violence, which is at its highest during the month of the election or immediately after, intra-party violence spikes prior to the general elections.

In Uganda, the pattern is clear prior to the elections of February 2016. Intra-party violence was particularly widespread in October 2015 when the ruling NRM held its primaries (Figure 1(d)). In Ghana, levels of violence are generally much lower with 79 recorded events across the five elections held during the period. Especially intra-party violence is rare and the patterns are generally a little murkier (see Figure 1(a)). However, the overall story is largely the same: In the years violence during elections is recorded, it takes the form of general election violence. Intra-party violence occurs either between elections or in the months prior to the elections in December 2012 and December 2016 (except one violent intra-party event recorded during the 2016 elections).

Figures 1(c) and (e) show that the temporal pattern is a little less discernable in South Africa and Zimbabwe. In general, both types of violence are common in the two cases with 1775 violent events in Zimbabwe and 660 in South Africa (Table 2). Although levels of general election violence are high around election time as expected, intra-party violence occurs in non-election years as much as in elections years. In South Africa, intra-party violence occurred prior to national as well as local elections in 2006, 2011, and 2016. This matches observer reports of increased violence within the ANC during selection of mayoral candidates as well as ensuing violent protests among citizens.[38]

Table 2. Distribution of election violence.

Country	General	Intra-party	Total
Ghana	63 (79.7%)	16 (20.3%)	79 (100%)
Uganda	100 (73.5%)	36 (26.5%)	136 (100%)
Kenya	159 (89.8%)	18 (10.2%)	177 (100%)
Zimbabwe	1691 (95.3%)	84 (4.7%)	1775 (100%)
South Africa	549 (83.2%)	111 (16.8%)	660 (100%)

In Zimbabwe, intra-party violence is much less common than general election violence (it accounts for 4.7%). In the first elections under investigation – in 2000 and 2002 – intra-party violence follows the expected pattern and spikes in the months prior to general elections. In recent years, intra-party violence has become much more frequent both outside and during elections. In 2014–2016, when intra-party violence is particularly frequent in Zimbabwe, the ongoing succession struggle in the ruling party, ZANU-PF, intensified as then leader Robert Mugabe turned 90 in 2014. The same year, the main opposition party, MDC, split in two following disagreements after its 2013 electoral defeat. This example shows that, as expected, not all intra-party violence is election related.

Despite these exceptions, intra-party violence in election years in the investigated countries does indeed tend to increase in the months prior to election campaigns, which – except in South Africa and Zimbabwe in the past few years – are generally the periods when intra-party violence is most frequent. In support of H1, there are indications that intra-party violence peaks during candidate selection, whereas inter-party violence sparks during the actual election campaign and continues into the electoral aftermath. After discussing the spatial patterns visible in the data, we formally test H1 below.

The spatial distribution of intra-party violence relative to inter-party violence indicates support for H2, which states that intra-party violence is more common where competitiveness is low. Uganda, a country completely dominated by Museveni's NRM, exhibits the highest share of intra-party violence. Across the three election periods, intra-party violence makes up more than a quarter of all violent events (Table 2). In Zimbabwe, where some districts are hotly contested between the ruling party and the opposition, intra-party violence makes up only 4.7% (Table 2). The pattern is not as clear in the investigated democracies. Intra-party violence is more common relative to inter-party violence under the ANC's dominant party rule in South Africa (16.8% of all events) than in the multi-party democracy of Kenya (10.2%) but slightly less common than in Ghana's multi-party system where intra-party violence accounts for 20.3% of all events. H2, which explores the importance of inter-party competitiveness for the distribution of inter- and intra-party violence, is formally tested below.

Temporal analysis: the timing of intra-party violence

H1 stated that whereas general election violence is most likely to occur during the election campaign and in the election's aftermath, intra-party violence will be most intense during individual parties' candidate nominations and thus occur prior to election day. The descriptive analysis of the data for individual countries lends support to this notion. We formally test the argument in a negative binomial regression model. The dependent variable is the frequency of violent events (per week) and the explanatory variable records the number of weeks to the next national level election. Because we expect this relationship to be nonlinear (that is, levels of violence increase and then drop as time passes), the squared and cubed terms of the countdown variable are included. To ensure that our findings are not driven by other confounding factors, we control for level of democracy,[39] urbanization,[40] and economic development.[41] We also include controls for general election violence (including temporally lagged versions)[42] in the models predicting intra-party violence and vice versa.[43] The results are presented in Table 3.[44]

Table 3. The timing of elections and violence 1998–2016.

	Dependent variable:	
	Intra-party (1)	General (2)
Weeks until election	−0.128**	−0.063**
	(0.028)	(0.009)
Weeks until election^2	0.001**	0.0004**
	(0.0003)	(0.0001)
Weeks until election^3	−0.00000**	−0.00000**
	(0.00000)	(0.00000)
General election violence	0.030	
	(0.032)	
General election violence t_{-1}	−0.132	
	(0.082)	
Intra-party violence		0.388
		(0.377)
Intra-party violence t_{-1}		0.541
		(0.372)
Level of democracy	−8.226**	−5.980**
	(2.935)	(0.830)
Urbanization	5.898	16.262**
	(4.208)	(1.384)
ln GDP per capital	1.582	−0.577*
	(1.040)	(0.318)
Observations	2,382	2,382
Log likelihood	−129.357	−1,421.248
Θ	0.328	0.206**
	(0.227)	(0.018)
Akaike inf. crit.	276.714	2,860.495

Note: Negative binomial regression. $*p < 0.1$; $**p < 0.05$; $***p < 0.01$.

As far as the likelihood of intra-party violence (Model 1), the number of weeks until the next election is statistically significant in the base-term, squared-term, and cubed-term. This confirms our expectation that the likelihood of intra-party violence is systematically and non-linearly related to election day. The model does not indicate at what point in the electoral cycle the risk of intra-party violence spikes. This pattern is revealed in Figure 2. Plot A illustrates that as more time passes and a new election approaches, the predicted frequency of intra-party violence becomes higher each week and peaks in the week before elections.[45] Immediately after elections, the predicted frequency of intra-party violence is low. This pattern is distinct from that of general election violence. As expected, general election violence also follows a distinct non-linear pattern (Table 3, Model 2). However, Figure 2 (Plot B) reveals that unlike intra-party violence, general election violence is almost as likely in the post-election as in the pre-election period.

The findings support H1: the temporal dynamic of intra-party violence is different from that of general election violence as intra-party violence occurs only prior to elections.

Notably, Table 3 reveals a distinct temporal and spatial pattern of intra-party violence. General election violence becomes more likely as urbanization increases while wealth and levels of democracy decrease but only increasing levels of democracy reduce the risk of intra-party violence. However, the effects of these country-level variables should be interpreted with caution as our sample consists of only five sub-Saharan African countries. Finally, it is noteworthy that in the five countries included in the sample, there is no clear link between intra-party violence and general election violence.

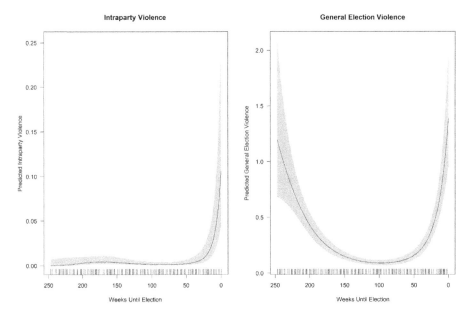

Figure 2. Effect of election timing on the use of violence by political parties.

With these results in mind, we turn to the spatial variation in intra-party violence and ask whether competitiveness can explain the frequency of intra-party violence.

Spatial analysis: intra-party violence and competitiveness across constituencies

The above analyses confirm the expectation that intra-party violence has its own distinct temporal dynamic. Its timing is different from that of general election violence as it primarily occurs prior to election day, and its causes are therefore also likely to be distinct. In the following section, we test H2, which states that whereas general election violence is commonly theorized to increase with levels of inter-party competitiveness, such competitiveness reduces the risk of intra-party violence. Intra-party violence, unlike general election violence, more commonly occurs where a single party dominates elections. In such dominant-party districts, violent conflict is likely to be relegated from election day, where the winner is typically known a priori, to the locally dominant party's nomination process.

As discussed, we expect the relationship between competitiveness and intra-party violence to play out on the constituency level as competitiveness varies across districts, and pockets of party dominance are common in Africa. In Kenya and Zambia, there is no nationally dominant party, but parties are dominant on the local level in many districts where the election winner is therefore often known a priori. This tendency is most common in majoritarian electoral systems with single-member districts.[46] Estimating the effect of competitiveness on the national level will mask the effects of locally dominant parties in a party system in which no party dominates most of the territory. We thus test H2 on the constituency level in Kenya and Zimbabwe.[47] The sample still includes a democracy and an autocracy, and both cases have sub-national variation on the degree of competitiveness as well as levels of intra-party violence. We do not claim that the results can be generalized across sub-Saharan Africa, but we do believe that they speak to the fact that patterns of intra-party violence may very well be driven by the same processes, regardless of regime type.

Table 4 presents the results of a negative binomial model of the constituency-level data for Zimbabwe and Kenya. The dependent variable is the weekly frequency of intra-party violence and general election violence respectively. The main explanatory variable is a measure of competitiveness based on the most recent parliamentary election.[48] It is calculated by subtracting the vote share for the runner-up from that of the winning candidate. To reverse the measure, this value is then subtracted from 1 so that higher values indicate higher levels of competitiveness.

We anticipate higher levels of competitiveness to be associated with more general election violence and less intra-party violence. The latter expectation should be especially true during the build-up to an election when parties are engaged in nominating candidates to run for office. As intra-party violence tends to occur in the months prior to elections and is very unlikely in the electoral aftermath, we include the timing variable (weeks until the next election) and interact it with the competitiveness measure. This allows us to explore the influence of competitiveness on intra-party violence at different points during the election cycle.[49] To simplify the model, we do not include the squared and cubed terms of the timing variable.

We include the same set of control variables as in Table 3 with one exception. To capture levels of economic development across districts, we overlay the intensity of nighttime lights and extract the mean value in each country (data from version 4.0

Table 4. Constituency-level competitiveness and violence, 1998–2016.

	Dependent variable:	
	Intra-party (1)	General (2)
Competitiveness	−2.664**	−0.674*
	(0.896)	(0.396)
Weeks until election	−0.031**	−0.003
	(0.008)	(0.002)
Competitiveness × weeks until election	0.031**	0.002
	(0.011)	(0.003)
General election violence	1.484*	
	(0.604)	
General election violence t_{-1}	2.025**	
	(0.583)	
Intra-party violence		2.239**
		(0.772)
Intra-party violence t_{-1}		2.195**
		(0.773)
Level of democracy	−6.283**	−12.054**
	(1.668)	(0.656)
Urbanization	0.210**	0.113**
	(0.059)	(0.021)
Nighttime lights	−7.703	−1.358
	(5.185)	(1.901)
Observations	168,500	168,500
Log likelihood	−528.155	−3,067.647
θ	0.005**	0.033**
	(0.002)	(0.004)
Akaike inf. crit.	1,074.309	6,153.293

Note: Negative binomial regression. *$p < 0.1$; **$p < 0.05$; ***$p < 0.01$.

of the DMSP-OLS Nighttime Lights Time Series[50]). Furthermore, we now measure competitiveness on the constituency level.

In model 1, the coefficient on weeks until the next election is negative and statistically significant, indicating that if the level of competitiveness is 0, the risk of intra-party violence will increase as the election approaches. This is in accordance with H1 and the results of Table 3.

More importantly, the results lend support to H2. The negative and significant coefficient on competitiveness shows that immediately prior to elections (when weeks until election = 0), inter-party competitiveness reduces the risk of intra-party violence as expected. The interaction effect between timing and competitiveness further tests H2. The positive and statistically significant effect indicates that as a country approaches election day (weeks until next election approaches 0), the negative effect of competitiveness on intra-party violence increases.[51]

The interaction term in model 2, exploring variation in the frequency of general election violence, has no statistically significant effect. Here, only the direct effect of competitiveness is significant. Contrary to expectations, it is negative, indicating that during elections (weeks until next election = 0), inter-party competitiveness reduces the risk of not only intra-party violence but also general election violence. This finding may reflect disagreement in the literature over whether competitiveness increases the risk of violence[52] or if violence is actually a strategy employed by weak opposition figures.[53] However, the coefficient should be interpreted with caution as the overall interaction effect is insignificant.

The results thus lend partial support to H2: competitiveness reduces the risk of intra-party violence, but the effect on general election violence is ambiguous. The relationship between competitiveness and intra-party violence is illustrated in Figure 3.

The figure shows the predicted frequency of intra-party violence as a function of constituency-level competition at four stages of the electoral cycle: one year prior, six months prior, three months prior, and one month prior. As expected, the frequency of intra-party violence decreases as competitiveness increases at all four points in time.[54] Furthermore, although the effect is present throughout the year prior to elections, the effect of competitiveness increases as an election approaches. Competitiveness reduces intra-party violence most effectively immediately prior to elections. This finding is intuitive as the intra-party violence occurring closest to elections is most likely to be related to the upcoming elections – rather than for instance succession struggles – and thus most likely to be affected by electoral competitiveness. Furthermore, competitiveness simply cannot affect the risk of intra-party violence in the periods (typically after elections) where such violence is absent. Thus, the spikes in intra-party violence immediately prior to elections in Zimbabwe and Kenya, illustrated in Figures 1(b) and (e), are likely accounted for by the electoral districts in which the winner is known a priori. In these districts, the actual competition does not occur between political parties on election day but within the dominant political party during candidate selection.

The constituency-level analysis also casts further light on the spatial patterns. Unlike in the state-level analyses in Table 3, patterns of intra- and inter-party violence across districts in Zimbabwe and Kenya are more similar. Urbanization increases the frequency of both intra-party and general election violence, whereas democracies tend to have fewer violent events (the latter variable is measured on the country level and should be interpreted with caution). The intensity of nighttime lights, proxying for

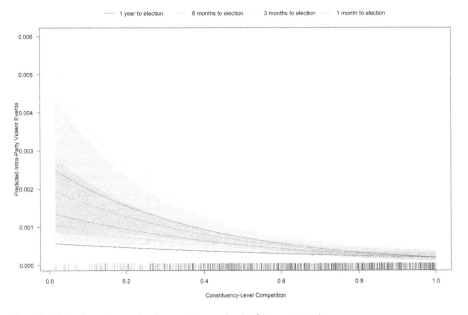

Figure 3. Effect of constituency-level competition on levels of intra-party violence.

economic development on the constituency level, does not affect the risk of general election violence or intra-party violence. At least in the case of Kenya and Zimbabwe, more developed constituencies are no less likely to see violence erupt. Most notably, general election violence and intra-party violence correlate on the district level. Districts with high levels of general election violence also tend to experience more intra-party violence and vice versa. Even though intra-party violence and general election violence have distinct temporal dynamics and competitiveness primarily affects intra-party violence, they also correlate. This finding may imply that there is a feedback loop between intra-party violence and general election violence. Such a relationship warrants greater attention by scholars in the future.

Conclusion

Although the study of election violence has expanded in recent years, research has focused exclusively on violence between members or supporters of different parties. We argue that this focus has led to a neglect of another important type of election violence: violence within political parties.

Using unique data of violent events that occur between supporters, members or candidates of the same political party for five sub-Saharan African countries between 1998 and 2016, we have brought attention to intra-party violence and shown that it is not a rare phenomenon. It occurs in both autocracies and democracies, making up as much as one-fifth of all violent events surrounding elections in some countries in our sample. Even in democratic countries such as South Africa and Ghana, violent events occur within political parties.

Our analyses also reveal that intra-party violence is distinct from inter-party violence and occurs according to its own specific dynamics. Whereas election violence generally spikes in the period surrounding election day and is common in the post-election period, intra-party violence tends to occur prior to elections. A large part of such violence is likely accounted for by the political parties' candidate selection procedures prior to elections. Analysing data on the sub-national level, we show that intra-party violence is more common in electoral districts where the winner is known a priori. In these cases, the power struggles do not take place on election day but during candidate nomination processes within the political party that is already known to win the elections. Thus, whereas less competitive elections have been known to be less susceptible to violence across political parties, as violent manipulation is unlikely to tilt the balance anyway, such elections may in fact not be less violent. Our results indicate that less competitive electoral contests see *more* intra-party violence.

It is important to reiterate that our sample covers five sub-Saharan African countries on the national level and only two on the sub-national level. As data become available, analyses should include more countries and regions. We believe, however, that our findings provide further justification for scholars to broaden the study of election violence to encompass other – and sometimes less visible – forms of violence.

The findings have implications for researchers on democratization and political violence as well as for those seeking to promote peaceful democratization. As researchers, we need to acknowledge that election violence occurs not only across but also within political parties and not only during and after election campaigns but also before they start. If we do not, we underestimate the problem of election violence and potentially misdiagnose its causes. As practitioners, we must bear in mind that any actions taken against electoral violence should not focus only on the campaign period and the electoral aftermath. Future efforts to prevent election violence should also take into account the candidate nomination processes within political parties. In this issue, Elklit and Wanyama and Seeberg, Wahman, and Skaaning discuss how the design and institutionalization of candidate selection processes may affect the risk of violence. Thus, considerations of electoral integrity[55] should stretch beyond the general election phase and into the very procedures of the political parties that contest elections.

Notes

1. Goldsmith, "Elections and Civil Violence"; Straus and Taylor, "Democratization and Electoral Violence"; Salehyan and Linebarger, "Elections and Social Conflict."
2. For example, Goldsmith, "Elections and Civil Violence."
3. Hafner-Burton, Hyde, and Jablonski, "When Do Governments Resort to Election Violence?"; Bhasin and Gandhi, "Timing and Targeting of State Repression."
4. Beaulieu, *Electoral Protest and Democracy*.
5. Fjelde and Höglund, "Electoral Institutions and Electoral Violence"; Salehyan and Linebarger, "Elections and Social Conflict."
6. See, for example, Wanyama et al., "Ethnicity And/Or Issues?"
7. Straus and Taylor, "Democratization and Electoral Violence"; Salehyan and Linebarger, "Elections and Social Conflict"; Wilkinson, *Votes and Violence*.
8. Straus and Taylor, "Democratization and Electoral Violence"; Salehyan and Linebarger, "Elections and Social Conflict"; Wilkinson, *Votes and Violence*.
9. Wilkinson, *Votes and Violence*; Höglund, Jarstad, and Kovacs, "The Predicament of Elections"; Fjelde and Höglund, "Electoral Institutions and Electoral Violence"; Salehyan and Linebarger, "Elections and Social Conflict"; Birch, "Electoral Systems and Electoral Misconduct."
10. Höglund, "Electoral Violence in Conflict-Ridden Societies."
11. Dunning, "Fighting and Voting"; Snyder, *From Voting to Violence*.

12. Salehyan and Linebarger, "Elections and Social Conflict"; Bhasin and Gandhi, "Timing and Targeting of State Repression."
13. Salehyan and Linebarger, "Elections and Social Conflict"; Bratton, "Vote Buying and Violence."
14. Straus and Taylor, "Democratization and Electoral Violence"; Wilkinson, *Votes and Violence*; Höglund, "Electoral Violence in Conflict-Ridden Societies"; Salehyan and Linebarger, "Elections and Social Conflict."
15. Hafner-Burton, Hyde, and Jablonski, "When Do Governments Resort to Election Violence?"; Salehyan and Linebarger, "Elections and Social Conflict."
16. Collier and Vicente, "Violence, Bribery, and Fraud."
17. Wahman, "Nationalized Incumbents and Regional Challengers."
18. Fox, "Bleak Future for Multi-Party Elections."
19. Wanyama et al., "Ethnicity And/Or Issues?"; see also Wanyama and Elklit on Kenya and Goldring and Wahman on Zambia in this issue.
20. Salehyan and Linebarger, "Elections and Social Conflict"; Straus and Taylor, "Democratization and Electoral Violence."
21. Fjelde and Höglund, "Electoral Institutions and Electoral Violence"; Birch, "Electoral Systems and Electoral Misconduct."
22. Höglund, Jarstad, and Kovacs, "The Predicament of Elections."
23. Höglund, "Electoral Violence in Conflict-Ridden Societies."
24. Straus and Taylor, "Democratization and Electoral Violence"; Bhasin and Gandhi, "Timing and Targeting of State Repression"; Hafner-Burton, Hyde, and Jablonski, "When Do Governments Resort to Election Violence?"; Beaulieu, *Electoral Protest and Democracy*; Kuhn, "Do Contentious Elections Trigger Violence?"
25. Raleigh et al., "Introducing ACLED."
26. Sundberg and Melander, "Introducing the UCDP Georeferenced Event Dataset."
27. Salehyan et al., "Social Conflict in Africa."
28. Straus and Taylor, "Democratization and Electoral Violence."
29. Hyde and Marinov, "Which Elections Can Be Lost?"
30. Coppedge et al., "V-Dem Codebook v6."
31. Norris et al., "The Expert Survey of Perceptions."
32. Zimbabwe Electoral Commission, "2013 Harmonized Elections Report."
33. A complete list of parties and keywords can be found in Online Appendix 1.
34. Online Appendix 2 details how coders distinguished intra-party violence from other forms of violence. It also includes illustrative examples of intra-party violent events found in the data.
35. Because we used several human coders, coder reliability was a concern. To explore the extent to which this may have been a problem, we had our coders independently code events that were scraped for the Kenyan case, which includes a mixture of inter-party (including riots/protests) and intra-party events. Of the 248 total events scraped from ACLED, our coders reported disagreement over seven events (2.8%). While coding the other cases, our coders worked together and discussed any events that were difficult to classify (often sitting side by side). We expect issues of coder reliability to be limited.
36. These comparisons can be found at http://www.acleddata.com/data/acled-version-7-1997-2016/.
37. Long et al., "Choosing Peace over Democracy."
38. *The Guardian*, "Two Shot Dead in Pretoria."
39. Democracy is the modified combined polity score (Marshall, Jaggers, and Gurr, "Polity IV Project") ranging from +10 (strongly democratic) to −10 (strongly autocratic).
40. The measure of urbanization is taken from version 2.0 of the PRIO-GRID data project (Tollefsen et al., "PRIO-GRID"). Based on Bontemps, Defourny, and Van Boegart ("Products Description and Validation Report"), it is the percentage of each grid cell that is covered by an urban area. To aggregate this to the state level, we take the mean value across the country.
41. This variable is the natural log of GDP per capita as found in the V-Dem data (Coppedge et al., "V-Dem Codebook v6").
42. We lag the violence variables because they vary weekly. The other control variables do not and thus do not warrant such treatment.
43. We also estimated the models without the country-level controls using negative binomial regression and fixed-effects. The models do not differ from what is presented in the manuscript.

44. Online Appendix 3 presents the results under two additional model specifications: robust standard errors clustered on the country and country fixed-effects. The only difference is when standard errors are clustered on the country. In this specification, the cubed-term of weeks until next election falls just short of statistical significance ($p = 0.12$). Importantly, however, the temporal pattern described in this article remains the same.
45. The bivariate relationship between the time until the next election and intra-party violence can be found in Online Appendix 5. Note that even though the prediction indicates a sharp increase in the weeks prior to the election, the bivariate plot reveals constant violence in the period prior to an election.
46. See, for example, Elklit and Wanyama and Goldring and Wahman in this issue.
47. The cases for which we have both competitiveness measures and the necessary spatial shapefiles.
48. From Wahman and Boone, "Captured Countryside?"
49. Leaving out the interaction would leave the model flawed as intra-party violence is extremely unlikely to occur in certain parts of the electoral cycle (see Figure 2) and we thus expect no effect of competitiveness at these points in time.
50. These data can be accessed using the following link: https://ngdc.noaa.gov/eog/dmsp/downloadV4composites.html. See also Mellander et al., "Night-Time Light Data," for a discussion of this proxy.
51. Online Appendix 4 presents the results under two alternative model specifications: robust standard errors clustered on the country and country fixed-effects. The results remain the same.
52. Straus and Taylor, "Democratization and Electoral Violence"; Salehyan and Linebarger, "Elections and Social Conflict"; Wilkinson, *Votes and Violence*.
53. Collier and Vicente, "Violence, Bribery, and Fraud."
54. The low severity predictions are the result of the large number of observations that result from looking at weekly patterns across constituencies.
55. Norris, *Why Elections Fail.*

Acknowledgements

The authors wish to thank Jessica Anderson, Colton Heffington, Michael Wahman, and the anonymous reviewers for very helpful comments on the manuscript.

Disclosure statement

No potential conflict of interest was reported by the authors.

Funding

This work was supported by Innovationsfonden [110-00002B].

Bibliography

Beaulieu, Emily. *Electoral Protest and Democracy in the Developing World.* New York: Cambridge University Press, 2014.

Bhasin, Tavishi, and Jennifer Gandhi. "Timing and Targeting of State Repression in Authoritarian Elections." *Electoral Studies*, Special Symposium: The new research agenda on electoral integrity 32, no. 4 (2013): 620–631.

Birch, Sarah. "Electoral Systems and Electoral Misconduct." *Comparative Political Studies* 40, no. 12 (2007): 1533–1556.

Bontemps, Sophie, Pierre Defourny, and Eric Van Boegart. "Products Description and Validation Report." European Space Agency, 2009. http://due.esrin.esa.int/files/GLOBCOVER2009_ Validation_Report_2.2.pdf

Bratton, Michael. "Vote Buying and Violence in Nigerian Election Campaigns." *Electoral Studies* 27, no. 4 (2008): 621–632.

Collier, Paul, and Pedro C. Vicente. "Violence, Bribery, and Fraud: The Political Economy of Elections in Sub-Saharan Africa." *Public Choice* 153, no. 1–2 (2012): 117–147.

Coppedge, Michael, John Gerring, Staffan I. Lindberg, Svend-Erik Skaaning, Jan Teorell, David Altman, Frida Andersson, et al. "V-Dem Codebook v6." Varieties of Democracy (V-Dem) Project 2016. https://www.v-dem.net/en/reference/version-6-mar-2016/.

Dunning, Thad. "Fighting and Voting: Violent Conflict and Electoral Politics." *Journal of Conflict Resolution* 55, no. 3 (2011): 327–339.

Fjelde, Hanne, and Kristine Höglund. "Electoral Institutions and Electoral Violence in Sub-Saharan Africa." *British Journal of Political Science* 46, no. 2 (2016): 297–320.

Fox, Roddy. "Bleak Future for Multi-Party Elections in Kenya." *The Journal of Modern African Studies* 34, no. 4 (1996): 597–607.

Goldsmith, Arthur A. "Elections and Civil Violence in New Multiparty Regimes: Evidence From Africa." *Journal of Peace Research* 52, no. 5 (2015): 607–621.

Hafner-Burton, Emilie M., Susan D. Hyde, and Ryan S. Jablonski. "When Do Governments Resort to Election Violence?" *British Journal of Political Science* 44, no. 1 (2014): 149–179.

Höglund, Kristine. "Electoral Violence in Conflict-Ridden Societies: Concepts, Causes, and Consequences." *Terrorism and Political Violence* 21, no. 3 (2009): 412–427.

Höglund, Kristine, Anna K. Jarstad, and Mimmi Söderberg Kovacs. 2009. "The Predicament of Elections in War-Torn Societies." *Democratization* 16, no. 3 (2009): 530–557.

Hyde, Susan, and Nikolay Marinov. "Which Elections Can Be Lost?" *Political Analysis* 20, no. 2 (2012): 191–210. doi:10.1093/pan/mpr040

Kuhn, Patrick. "Do Contentious Elections Trigger Violence?" In *In Contentious Elections. From Ballots to Barricades*, edited by Pippa Norris, Richard W. Frank, and Ferran Martínez i Coma, 89–110. New York: Routledge, 2015.

Long, James D., Karuti Kanyinga, Karen E. Ferree, and Clark Gibson. 2013. "Choosing Peace Over Democracy." *Journal of Democracy* 24, no. 3 (2013): 140–155. doi:10.1353/jod.2013.0048

Marshall, Monty, Keith Jaggers, and Ted Gurr. "Polity IV Project." Center for Systemic Peace, 2011. http://www.systemicpeace.org/polity/polity4.htm

Mellander, C., J. Lobo, K. Stolarick, and Z. Matheson. "Night-Time Light Data: A Good Proxy Measure for Economic Activity?" *PLoS ONE* 10, no. 10 (2015): e0139779.

Norris, Pippa. *Why Elections Fail*. New York: Cambridge University Press, 2015.

Norris, Pippa, Ferran Martínez i Coma, Alessandro Nai, and Max Groemping. 2016. "The Expert Survey of Perceptions of Electoral Integrity, PEI_4.0." 2015. www.electoralintegrityproject.com. http://Thedata.harvard.edu/Dvn/Dv/PEI

Raleigh, Clionadh, Andrew Linke, Håvard Hegre, and Joakim Karlsen. "Introducing ACLED: An Armed Conflict Location and Event Dataset Special Data Feature." *Journal of Peace Research* 47, no. 5 (2010): 651–660.

Salehyan, Idean, Cullen S. Hendrix, Jesse Hamner, Christina Case, Christopher Linebarger, Emily Stull, and Jennifer Williams. "Social Conflict in Africa: A New Database." *International Interactions* 38, no. 4 (2012): 503–511.

Salehyan, Idean, and Christopher Linebarger. "Elections and Social Conflict in Africa, 1990–2009." *Studies in Comparative International Development* 50, no. 1 (2014): 23–49.

Snyder, Jack L. *From Voting to Violence: Democratization and Nationalist Conflict*. New York, NY: W. W. Norton & Company, 2000.

Straus, Scott, and Charles Taylor. "Democratization and Electoral Violence in SSA, 1990-2008." In *Voting in Fear*, edited by Dorina Bekoe, 15–38. Washington, DC: United States Institute of Peace Press, 2012.

Sundberg, Ralph, and Erik Melander. "Introducing the UCDP Georeferenced Event Dataset." *Journal of Peace Research* 50, no. 4 (2013): 523–532.

The Guardian. "Two Shot Dead in Pretoria as Violence Flares over ANC Mayoral Candidate," June 22, 2016.

Tollefsen, Andreas Forø, Håvard Strand, and Halvard Buhaug. "PRIO-GRID: A Unified Spatial Data Structure." *Journal of Peace Research* 49, no. 2 (2012): 363–374.

Wahman, Michael. "Nationalized Incumbents and Regional Challengers: Opposition- and Incumbent-Party Nationalization in Africa." *Party Politics* 23, no. 3 (2017): 309–322.

Wahman, Michael, and Catherine Boone. "Captured Countryside? Stability and Change in Sub-National Support for African Incumbent Parties." *Journal of Comparative Politics* 50, no. 2 (2018): 189–216.

Wanyama, Frederick O., Jørgen Elklit, Bodil Folke Frederiksen, and Preben Kaarsholm. "Ethnicity And/Or Issues? The 2013 General Elections in Western Kenya." *Journal of African Elections* 13, no. 2 (2014): 169–195.

Wilkinson, Steven I. *Votes and Violence: Electoral Competition and Ethnic Riots in India.* Cambridge: Cambridge University Press, 2006.

Zimbabwe Electoral Commission. "2013 Harmonized Elections Report." 2013. http://www.zec.gov.zw/download/category/78-report

The Party Paradox: a Comment (February 20, 2018)

Nicolas van de Walle

ABSTRACT
This article analyzes several stylized facts and implications concerning intra-party violence developed in the other articles of this special issue on intra-party violence in African electoral systems. It then turns more specifically to the implications of intra-party violence for democratic consolidation in the region, and argues that paradoxically, though parties are centrally important to democratic politics, the degree to which they are internally inclusive and participatory may not have much importance, or may indeed undermine democracy. Though they are perhaps the key actor on the path to a consolidated democracy, they tend to work best when they themselves are not internally democratic.

Introduction

The focus in this special issue on the internal nomination process within African political parties and the proclivity for intra-party violence is particularly welcome because we still know so little about the internal dynamics of parties in the region. The data and qualitative information in the preceding articles on this developing dimension of African party politics are rich in implications for both party politics and African democratization. Most of the literature on electoral violence has implicitly focused on conflict between political parties. By documenting significant violence within political parties and the different logic it has, these article impose a reconsideration of electoral violence.

In this brief note, I draw out several stylized facts and implications concerning intra-party violence during the nomination process, from this special issue. I then turn more specifically to the implications of the findings for democratic consolidation in the region, and argue that paradoxically, though parties are centrally important to democratic politics, the degree to which they are internally inclusive and participatory may not have much importance, or may indeed undermine democracy.

Candidate nomination and violence

The preceding articles allow for several generalizations and suggest several important implications. First, the authors show that, in sharp contrast to inter-party violence, intra-party violence is more likely to occur in non-competitive elections, and usually well before the election.[1] Gaining one's party's nomination is the key step for prospective candidates for office in dominant party systems such as Uganda, Tanzania, or South Africa, three countries covered in the issue, since the candidate of the incumbent party is pretty much assured a victory in the main election.

In more competitive party systems, winning the party primary would be more likely to be followed by defeat in the general election, and so the presence of violence at the nomination stage of the electoral process is testimony to the absence of real party competition in these dominant party systems. In many cases, the dominant party nomination process actually resembles the primary process that existed before the wave of democratization resulted in the legalization of opposition parties. In the old single party days as well, the real competition concerned the right to represent the government party, and could be quite vicious, even if less likely to be widely reported.[2] In addition, the articles on Kenya and Zambia suggest that non-competitive individual legislative races are also more likely to generate violence.[3] Reeder and Seeberg characterize the latter examples of violence as resulting from "party dominance" at the district level,[4] but the key causal mechanism is as much the competitiveness of the election as it is the characteristic of the party involved.

One implication of this proclivity to violence in dominant party primaries is to highlight once again the role of state-funded clientelism in African politics. The electoral offices of parties likely to win control of the state are almost certainly worth more to candidates than is the case for opposition parties, whose office holders will benefit from signally smaller "spoils". Thus, the higher stakes of competition for the incumbent party probably result in more hard-fought primary campaigns that are more likely to result in violence. Goldring and Wahman's finding for Zambia that primaries for "open seats", where the member of parliament (MP) does not stand for re-election, were statistically more likely to result in violence is significant in this respect.[5]

A second stylized fact is that much of this violence reveals deep-seated factionalism within parties that appear often to be constituted by little more than segmented coteries of groups that are united neither by interest nor by ideology. Political entrepreneurs compete for legislative office out of personal ambition largely unconstrained by party norms of collegiality or fair play. Factionalism is a common ailment in political parties all over the world, but it is less likely to result in dysfunctional practices such as those noted in the preceding articles when it exists within more institutionalized parties than most of the ones prevailing in Africa. The exceptions are instructive and worth noting: MacGiollabhui's article on the African National Congress (ANC) in South Africa demonstrates that a more institutionalized party can process substantial policy-based and personal contentiousness without falling prey to violence.[6]

Third, then, nomination violence testifies to the low level of institutionalization of most African parties. In sum, the articles show that party hierarchies either lack the capacity to select candidates, or they are unable to adequately regulate the process of nomination and enforce the rules in place, once they have decided to open up the process to some degree of popular participation. That decision may, indeed, be forced upon them by their inability to exert top-down control over local party actors, with established procedures and norms for candidate nomination.

In countries like Uganda or Kenya, and in sharp distinction to the ANC in South Africa, the weakness of procedural norms politicizes nomination processes. Many if not most African parties delegate the mobilization of voters over much of the national territory to local brokers over which they do not necessarily exert much control. The prevalence of brokerage is of course a symptom of a low level of organizational discipline and capacity.

In turn, issues of state capacity reinforce the low levels of party institutionalization to make violence more likely. The professionalism of the police and the judiciary in particular shape the likelihood of violence. When it is low, violence is less likely to be sanctioned and will thus be more common.

Fourth, though perhaps less comprehensively treated by the articles, the mode of nomination probably affects the likelihood of violence. The more closed and or top-down the process of nomination, the less likely the amount of violence. In the ideal, textbook Leninist party fully applying "democratic centralism", followers may offer their opinion in a relatively open manner, including on candidate nomination, but the decision is made by the hierarchy and brooks no dissent once it has been made. The more participatory the processes, the likelier violence will occur, everything else being equal, and the broader the violence is likely to be. All political parties are likely to incorporate divergent interests, but the more centralized the decision-making, the less likely conflict will result in open violence. Arguably, highly centralized parties might be viewed as generating contestation from members who are excluded from decision-making, but this seems more likely to result in exit than in voice, as the excluded will be tempted to establish their own separate parties, or join alternative existing ones, in which their voices garner more influence.

In sum, intra-party violence during the nomination process is revealing of the current state of parties and party systems in the region in a number of important respects. If we think of parties as essential to democracy, what are the implications of the rise of intra-party violence for democracy and democratic deepening in the region? In their introduction, Seeberg et al. argue that this violence "threatens to derail processes of democratization and undermine the consolidation of democracy". This seems incontrovertible in so far as any kind of political violence undermines stability and more specifically electoral politics, though the impact of violence on electoral politics is notoriously difficult to ascertain.[7] Seeberg and her colleagues do not find that this intra-party violence is correlated with level of democracy, since their survey of African countries finds this violence in both more and less democratic countries. But this conclusion contrasts with the argument in MacGiollabhui's articles on the ANC in South Africa that argues that that party's internal democratic procedures have had a positive impact on democratic consolidation in the country. Is that a generalizable finding or is it linked to South Africa's distinctive democratization trajectory? I turn to examining the link between internal party governance and democracy.

The ambiguous role of political parties

The evidence presented in the preceding articles is, on the contrary, evidence for the truth of a central paradox about the political role of parties: though they are perhaps the key actor on the path to a consolidated democracy, they tend to work best when they themselves are not internally democratic; and I link this to a broader paradox regarding the reliance of democratic regimes on non-majoritarian institutions and organizations. This is a difficult lesson, given the premium placed on political participation in the contemporary era, but it is one with important theoretical and practical implications for democratic consolidation.

Two venerable political scientists have long shaped most of the debates about the interaction between democracy and political parties. E. E. Schattschneider's often-quoted remark has it that "political parties created democracy and modern democracy is unthinkable save in terms of the parties".[8] Parties are both a necessary form of organization to mobilize voters and compete for electoral office, and they inevitably structure and give coherence to legislative life. But equally well known, though lacking the single pithy quote by which to be remembered, is Michels' "iron law of oligarchy",[9] that argued that modern political parties (and indeed all large complex organizations) were necessarily non-democratic in their internal governance, given the inexorable professionalization of the party bureaucracy. Note that Michels was making an empirical statement rather than a normative one. He believed that efforts to democratize complex organizations were bound to fail, as leaders would always be able to apply the resources the organization provided them with to counter dissent and manipulate the rank and file. This proposition would not be considered particularly counter-intuitive for most complex organizations – no one really expects a big private corporation like, say, General Motors to be democratically managed, but it has generally been viewed as controversial in the case of political parties, given their participatory rhetoric and democratic electoral aspirations. Michels was moreover writing at a time when large membership-based parties were emerging in Europe that claimed to be faithful representatives of the views of their rank and file members.

Political parties are critically important to the functioning of democracy, yet the most successful parties are in fact not necessarily internally democratic in many if not most of their processes. This is the central paradox about political parties. Indeed, one could go further and suggest that political parties are more likely to play the critical role they are ascribed for democratic consolidation in recent democracies if and when they are not internally democratic.

Taking this paradox further, my argument is that democratic deepening in fledgling democracies may well be advanced by the presence of a pluralistic and competitive party system, in which the incumbent party is not favoured by the rules of the game, and opposition parties do not face an "uneven playing field"; but it is not advanced by intra-party democracy. Participatory processes within the party, such as primaries, are likely to divide parties, undermine party discipline, confuse voters and – as suggested in these articles – cause political violence.

Arguments for more intra-party democracy

Four arguments are usually advanced on behalf of greater popular participation in intra-party decision-making. A first argument is that opening up the process will make the party more attractive to voters and thus promote the party's electoral prospects. This is either because competition is valued for its positive effects, notably in improving the quality of candidates, who will be suitably "tested" by the competition; or because it is believed that participation will be popular and expand turnout. Indeed, the opening up of party primaries in west-European countries was explicitly designed to enhance turn out; as Van Biezen et al. argue "The logic here seems to be that the more widely based the selectorate, the greater will be the chances that the candidates and leaders who are chosen will have a far-reaching appeal".[10]

At least in part, the rationale to open parties up has its origins in the kind of deep-seated scepticism about political parties that is a long-standing western intellectual tradition, going back to the eighteenth century, and elegantly described by Madison or Jefferson in the American context, in which party leaders are viewed as systematically likely to undermine the public good unless they are constrained.

The empirical evidence from western democracies that intra-party democracy increases popular participation and turnout is actually weak,[11] though the counterfactual is hard to establish in the countries that did undertake these reforms, because parties there typically were suffering from declining voter enthusiasm before the reforms. It is hard to dismiss the possibility that reforms in favour of greater internal participation in fact slowed down the ongoing decline of turnout and party membership.

Parties in the new low-income democracies are probably particularly attracted to the promise of increasing their participatory processes. Very few of them have a substantial number of members, unlike the mass parties emerging in Europe observed by Michels. Even long-standing African parties, in contrast, lack a base in the union movement or in organized religions, the pillars of mass parties in western Europe in the early twentieth century. Most parties in the region are moreover not long-standing. A handful of dominant parties – one thinks of the CCM in Tanzania, or FRELIMO in Mozambique, in addition to the ANC in South Africa discussed by MacGiollabhui in this issue, which have dominated the political scene for decades and have invested in organizational capacity and a popular presence throughout the territory, but they remain exceptions.[12] Even incumbent parties that have recently won large legislative majorities typically do not enjoy substantial numbers of rank-and-file members.

In addition, attitudinal surveys such as the Afrobarometer consistently find that political parties are generally unpopular and distrusted by voters, who view them at best as a necessary evil. In these circumstances, opening up the decision-making process within the party as a way to improve the party's image and gain members must be very tempting, even if the party leaders may believe they will be able to control and channel this participation.

Indeed, buttressing this view that it is likely to be popular, the second argument for greater participation is the normative one that argues that greater internal democracy is inherently the good policy, regardless of its outcomes. As Rohrschneider has argued, in western political parties, particularly on the left, the ideological bias in favour of internal party democracy and greater participation by party members has grown in recent years.[13]

It is striking in this respect that western aid to political parties in Africa has generally promoted greater transparency and participation. For example, the international work on political parties by the National Democratic Institute in the United States (US) seems remarkably sanguine about participatory processes in the parties of fledgling democracies.[14] Though it does recognize some potential risks of intra-party democracy, much of the empirical material comes from long-standing democracies in western Europe, and the possibility of violence as a result of greater participation is never discussed.

A third argument on behalf of greater participation in political parties is linked closely to this normative argument. It argues that parties constitute schools for citizen behaviour and that democratic internal party processes provide opportunities to help improve citizenship among voters.[15] Participating in electoral processes, whether as a member of a political party, or as an electoral observer, or even a journalist covering the election, almost certainly provides knowledge about them.

An old debate pits political scientists who view political parties as instruments of democracy with those who argue that parties and their behaviour are mostly merely symptomatic of the state of democracy so that parties in more democratic countries will tend to demonstrate greater respect for democracy.[16] One does not have to fully subscribe to this latter view, to view with scepticism the "school of democracy" argument. After all, the primary function of political parties and a prerequisite for their very survival is the ability to win elections.[17] Regardless of their other virtues, parties that do not win electoral offices are destined to fade away, particularly in the young democracies of low-income countries, where parties cannot rely on public funding to compete in elections. As a result, the school for citizenship argument may constitute an argument for internal party democracy, but is unlikely to constitute a compelling incentive for parties to open up their internal processes, since improving the citizenship of their members will always be a very secondary motivation to winning elections.

Moreover, competing effectively in elections should provide ample motivation for parties to buttress their internal organizational performance, since the alternative is defeat and having to survive in the political wilderness, no easy feat in low-income countries. On the other hand, the evidence suggests opening up participation in young parties may actually undermine their limited organizational capacity, an issue to which we now turn.

Fourth, and finally, intra-party democracy might be promoted as a desirable substitute for low levels of inter-party democracy, in low-income electoral systems. In electoral autocracies, in particular, it could be argued that internal party democracy would be an important palliative, which might in time build the momentum for greater democracy. Interestingly, in Africa and elsewhere, the elimination of a political opposition was once legitimated with the argument that the internal democracy of the single party made an opposition unnecessary. In an early defence of the single party, for instance, Tanzanian President Julius Nyerere argued that

> where there is one party, provided that it is identified with the nation as a whole, the foundations of democracy can be firmer, and the people can have more opportunity to exercise a real choice, than where you have two or more parties.[18]

The absence of real party competition may indeed make intra-party democracy more desirable, but it will not make it more likely, as suggested by the long history of the single party in Africa and elsewhere. On the contrary, scholars such as Riedl and LeBas have recently cogently argued that inter-party competition in Africa has been the main motor of party institutionalization processes.[19] It is competition and conflict across parties that play the key role in strengthening them.

Participation and organizational capacity

To these criticisms, it might be countered that the key factor influencing the likelihood of intra-party violence is the organizational capacity of the party, rather than the degree of participation allowed in the party. If the nomination process and decision-making rules are well institutionalized, participation will not prove to be dysfunctional.

The evidence from relatively more capacious parties in the west suggests otherwise. The American context is instructive. It is common for American observers to regret the impact of the post-Watergate reforms in the 1970s, increasing transparency and greater popular participation in both the Republican and Democratic parties, in response to both the decline of their popularity and internal scandals that plagued both parties.

It is true that these reforms did not bring about actual intra-party violence. Yet, many observers have expressed at least some nostalgia for the bad old days of nominations being decided by "old white men in smoke-filled back rooms", which they argue resulted in better nominees, with greater chances of winning, as well as less ideologically extreme ones. The less savoury procedures paradoxically produced better outcomes.

Much the same kinds of dynamics can be viewed in Europe, where in addition to declining membership and popularity, the traditional parties have been forced to evolve by the threat they face from new parties.[20] Parties there too have sought to enhance the power of their members, and with equally mixed results. In the 2017 French elections, for instance, the resort to competitive rank-and-file presidential primaries was criticized by leaders of both the Socialist and Republican parties for similar reasons: not only did the two candidates chosen fail to reach the second round of the presidential election that witnessed the triumph of Emmanuel Macron and his En Marche party, but in addition, the primary and subsequent electoral collapse exacerbated long-standing divisions in both parties, which exploded into rival factions soon after the election.

It is true that other observers like Cohen et al. have argued that the post-Watergate reforms have not prevented the continued dominance of top-down processes, in which, in the end, "the party decides", rather than American primary voters.[21] But note that Cohen et al.'s argument is rather different than Michels' since they argue that it is not the bureaucratic power of the party leadership, but rather their ability to frame the ideational choices and dominate the electoral discourse that leads them to continue to decide who will be the nominees.

Some European observers of parties have argued that central party elites have sometimes believed that open primaries would serve their interests by weakening local rank-and-file party members, even as they empowered voters, particularly in open primaries.[22] This dynamic, indeed, seems to be relevant to the African cases discussed in this issue. The article on Zambia views "center–periphery" dynamics as characteristic of intra-party conflict, with violence often resulting from the clumsy machinations of party leaders outside of the district.

The claim that organizational capacity matters more to the impact of parties than the degree of internal democracy fails to recognize the extent to which organizational capacity may actually be undermined by greater participation. Thus, to return to the American case, even if one accepts that the Republican Party establishment "decided" the nomination of Donald Trump in the 2016 US elections,[23] it seems clear that the Republican establishment was deeply divided about Trump's candidacy. The internal divisions of the party were directly responsible for his nomination: a less fractured party that was less decentralized and tolerant of independent political entrepreneurship than the main American political parties would not have selected a candidate like Donald Trump.

In less institutionalized parties than the main American parties, intra-party democracy is more likely to produce worst outcomes than simply incompetent or vulgar candidates. As suggested by the preceding articles, the weakly defined formal party procedures and norms within the nomination process are much more likely to be undermined by an increase in participation, notably involving clientelism, corruption, and perhaps violence. Even in Ghana, perhaps the region's most institutionalized party system, Ichino and Nathan argue that the prevailing clientelistic logic of Ghanaian politics conditions the distinctive effects of primaries on both incumbent and opposition parties, and only the latter probably benefit.[24]

In his assessment of internal democracy in the ANC, MacGiollabhui makes the argument that the party's inclusive spirit has been key in stabilizing intra-party competition; indeed, the party has proven impressively adept at reconciling substantial policy disagreements relatively peacefully with the use of relatively inclusive internal procedures. Yet, again, the counter-factual is not easy to establish. After all, the ANC built its strength over several decades under Apartheid with much less inclusive procedures, imposed on it by political repression and the exile or imprisonment of most of its leaders. Today, the corruption, clientelism and complacency that have evidently gangrened the ANC suggest a deeply dysfunctional party, held together in large part by its glorious past and the advantages of incumbency.

Admittedly, the possibility cannot be dismissed that internal participatory processes will in the long run create dynamics within African parties to build up their capacity and push greater institutionalization of party procedures. Interestingly, such a longitudinal trend is not discussed in any of the articles in this issue. If anything, they tend to view the problem of violence as one that has progressively increased over time. It is important in this respect to avoid the functionalist fallacy that institutions develop because they are desirable, and we must ask who will benefit from such participatory processes? In fact, in so far as institutionalization is a public good and thus vulnerable to free-riding, it is more likely to develop if its benefits can be captured by one actor or a well-organized faction within the party. Indeed, this may explain why fake and façade participatory rituals that serve the interests of the leadership litter the history of party development.

Thus, the final argument against intra-party democracy in low-income electoral systems may be that it is not only unlikely to promote better electoral results, it may actually serve to weaken the party and its efforts to build party organizational capacity.

Conclusion: democracy's reliance on non-majoritarian institutions

I have suggested that the prevalence of intra-party violence in Africa documented in this special issue argues against competitive and open nomination processes, at least in part because the evidence that they promote democratization is quite weak. The articles provide evidence that open nomination processes reflect party weakness even as they also help to perpetuate them. In that sense, African party leaders may not have much choice but to adopt inclusive primaries. Nonetheless, these processes should not be justified as desirable because of an alleged effect of promoting democracy. In the low-income fledgling electoral regimes of Africa, inter-party parity and competition benefit democracy; more transparent and participatory intra-party decision-making does not.

This party paradox should be understood to be part of a larger paradox about liberal democracy, which is that many of its components are not democratic in a meaningful sense. Of course, modern democratic institutions rarely completely embody the simple principles of direct democracy. Popular referenda are surprisingly rare and almost all elected officials have fixed terms and rules that limit the ability of popular opinion to usurp the delegation of authority to the official conferred by elections. Impeachment of elected officials is usually procedurally difficult and designed to be rare and exceptional. The duration of terms of office are overwhelmingly four or five years, and few legislative offices are saddled with term limits, which would undo incumbency advantages. In sum, Democratic constitutional theorists going back to the eighteenth century have consistently worried about the dangers of direct democracy – the threat of "the mob" – and their efforts to protect elected officials from popular pressures other than during well-spaced elections anchors most modern democratic constitutions, with remarkably few exceptions.[25]

But in addition, most democratic constitutions routinely delegate to non-majoritarian institutions key democratic functions in the judicial and executive branch of government, with a logic that is widely accepted as legitimate across most democracies. For instance, the need to protect the justice system from the passions of citizens is widely accepted, and this third branch of government is routinely led by non-elected officials with long terms of office. It is similarly widely viewed as generally positive that a number of activities in the executive branch of government be insulated from political pressures that would negatively influence their performance. In most long-standing democracies, central bankers and their economic policies are shielded and not immediately accountable to voters, thanks notably to long terms of office. Similarly, technocratic regulatory commissions or specific investigatory bodies are protected from criticism in most countries.

These non-majoritarian institutions are justified in two somewhat contradictory ways. On the one hand, they are viewed as protecting key functions from popular participatory pressures. But, in addition, they are viewed as desirable because they serve to protect institutions from the abuses of the executive and legislative branch of government, and thus actually and paradoxically serve the interests of democracy. In some cases, these two arguments are similar – the executive and legislative branches are viewed as particularly vulnerable to popular pressures. But in other cases, they are not. Instead, constitutionalist arguments suggest that certain key functions of government not be manipulated for partisan advantage or even for reasons of executive power. Thus, the independence of the Central Bank is viewed as a way to avoid incumbent executives unsustainably printing up currency in the run up to elections.

It might be argued that some of these non-majoritarian institutions are either not necessary or not desirable. Some have been criticized, as when scholars have argued that the policy arguments for an independent Central Bank are not well-founded.[26] But such debates have rarely been engaged in in the recent democracies of the Third Wave, where the stakes are higher, not least because the sirens of populism are viewed as louder and the possibility of executive abuses of power greater.

As for political parties, it is important to recognize that internal transparency and popular participation do not necessarily serve the cause of democracy. The articles in this special issue demonstrate the priorities that African parties need to adopt if they are to compete effectively and peacefully for office. Normative reasons on behalf of greater inclusion may be compelling, but the prevalence of nomination violence in African parties suggests that the relationship between internal party democracy and national democratic consolidation is tenuous at best.

Instead, my conclusion from this special issue is that the better way to serve the cause of democratization is to promote party organization and state capacity, notably in the state institutions that are best able to sanction and limit violence. Ultimately, effective law and order institutions constitute the best insurance against violence and impunity. Moreover, no real alternatives exist to the difficult but necessary task of building greater inter-party parity and a level playing field for the opposition. Whether parties make their decisions in smoky back rooms or in inclusive primaries will ultimately prove less important to building democracy.

Notes

1. See Reeder and Seeberg, "Fighting your Friends," 2018.
2. Hermet, *Elections without Choice*.
3. Wanyama and Elklit, "Nomination Violence in Kenya"; and Goldring and Wahman, "Fighting for a Name," 2018.
4. Reeder and Seeberg, "Fighting your Friends." 2018.
5. Goldring and Wahman, "Fighting for a Name." 2018.
6. MacGiollabhui, "Battleground," 2018.
7. Bratton, "Vote Buying and Violence"; Collier and Vincente, "Votes and Violence"; and Bekoe and Burchard, "The Contradictions of Pre-Election Violence."
8. Schattschneider, *Party Government*, 1.
9. Michels, *Political Parties*.
10. Van Biezen, Mair, and Poguntke, "Going, Going … Gone," 40.
11. Scarrow, "Parties and the Expansion of Direct Democracy."
12. Bleck and van de Walle, *Electoral Politics in Africa*, Chapter 4.
13. Rohrschneider, "How Iron is the Iron Law?"
14. See for instance, Scarrow, *Implementing Intra-Party Democracy*; and Ashiagbor, *Selecting Candidates for Legislative Office*.
15. Scarrow, *Implementing Intra-Party Democracy*, 3.
16. For instance, Stokes, "Political Parties and Democracy."
17. See Aldrich, *Why Parties?*; and Stokes, "Political Parties and Democracy."
18. Nyerere, "Democracy and the Party System," 200.
19. Riedl, *Authoritarian Origins*; and LeBas, *From Protest to Parties*.
20. Berman, "The Life of the Party."
21. Cohen et al., *The Party Decides*. See also Hassell, "Party Control."
22. See for instance, Sandri, Seddone, and Venturino, *Party Primaries*, 6–7.
23. Friedersdorf, "How the Party Decided."
24. Ichino and Nathan, "Do Primaries Improve Electoral Performance?"
25. See Brennan, *Against Democracy*, for an important recent statement of similar views.
26. See McNamara, "Rational Fictions"; Thatcher and Sweet, "Theory and Practice of Delegation."

Disclosure statement

No potential conflict of interest was reported by the author.

Bibliography

Aldrich, J. H. *Why Parties? The Origin and Transformation of Political Parties in America*. Chicago: University of Chicago Press, 1995.
Ashiagbor, S. *Political Parties and Democracy in Theoretical and Practical Perspectives. Selecting Candidates for Legislative Office*. Washington, DC: National Democratic Institute, 2008.
Bekoe, D. A., and S. M. Burchard. "The Contradictions of Pre-Election Violence: The Effects of Violence on Voter Turnout in Sub-Saharan Africa." *African Studies Review*, 60, no. 2 (2017): 73–92.
Berman, S. "The Life of the Party." *Comparative Politics*. 30, no. 1 (1997): 101–122.
Bleck, J., and N. van de Walle. *Electoral Politics in Africa since 1990: Continuity in Change*. New York: Cambridge University Press, 2018.
Bratton, M. "Vote Buying and Violence in Nigerian Election Campaigns." *Electoral Studies*, 27, no. 4 (2008): 621–632.

Brennan, J. *Against Democracy*. Princeton, NJ: Princeton University Press, 2017.

Cohen, M., D. Karol, H. Noel, and J. Zaller. *The Party Decides: Presidential Nominations Before and After Reform*. Chicago, IL: University of Chicago Press, 2009.

Collier, P., and P. C. Vicente. "Votes and Violence: Evidence From a Field Experiment in Nigeria." *The Economic Journal*, 124, no. 574 (2014): 324–355.

Friedersdorf, C. "How the Party Decided on Trump." *The Atlantic*, May 3, 2016.

Goldring, Edward and M. Wahman. "Fighting for a name on the ballot: constituency-level analysis of nomination violence in Zambia." *Democratization*. 25, no. 6 (2018): 996–1015.

Hassell, H. J. "Party Control of Party Primaries: Party Influence in Nominations for the US Senate." *The Journal of Politics* 78, no. 1 (2016): 75–87.

Hermet, G. *Elections Without Choice*. Berlin: Springer, 1978.

Ichino, N., and N. L. Nathan. "Do Primaries Improve Electoral Performance? Clientelism and Intra-Party Conflict in Ghana." *American Journal of Political Science* 57, no. 2 (2013): 428–441.

LeBas, A. *From Protest to Parties: Party-Building and Democratization in Africa*. Oxford: Oxford University Press, 2013.

Mac Giollabhui, Shane. "Battleground: candidate sleection and violence in Africa's dominant political parties." *Democratization*. 25, no. 6 (2018): 978–995.

McNamara, K. "Rational Fictions: Central Bank Independence and the Social Logic of Delegation." *West European Politics*, 25, no. 1 (2002): 47–76.

Michels, R. *Political Parties: A Sociological Study of the Oligarchical Tendencies of Modern Democracy*. New York: The Free Press, 1915.

Nyerere, J. "Democracy and the Party System." In *Freedom and Unity: A Selection From Speeches and Writings, 1952–1963*, 195–203. London: Oxford University Press, 1966.

Reeder, Bryce W. and M. Seeberg. "Fighting your friends? A study of intra-party violence in sub-Saharan Africa." *Democratization*. 25, no. 6 (2018): 1033–1051.

Riedl, R. B. *Authoritarian Origins of Democratic Party Systems in Africa*. New York: Cambridge University Press, 2014.

Rohrschneider, R. "How Iron is the Iron Law of Oligarchy?" *European Journal of Political Research* 25 (1994): 207–238.

Sandri, Giulia, Antonella Seddone, and Fulvio Venturino, eds. *Party Primaries in Comparative Perspective*. Farnham: Ashgate Publishing, Ltd., 2015.

Scarrow, S. E. "Parties and the Expansion of Direct Democracy: Who Benefits?" *Party Politics* 5, no. 3 (1990): 341–362.

Scarrow, S. E. *Political Parties and Democracy in Theoretical and Practical Perspectives: Implementing Intra-Party Democracy*. Washington, DC: National Democratic Institute for International Affairs, 2005.

Schattschneider, E. E. *Party Government*. New York: Holt, Rinehart and Winston, 1941.

Stokes, S. C. "Political Parties and Democracy." *Annual Review of Political Science* 2, no. 1 (1999): 243–267.

Thatcher, M., and A. S. Sweet. "Theory and Practice of Delegation to Non-Majoritarian Institutions." *West European Politics* 25, no. 1 (2002): 1–22.

Van Biezen, I., P. Mair, and T. Poguntke. "Going, Going, … Gone? The Decline of Party Membership in Contemporary Europe." *European Journal of Political Research* 51, no. 1 (2012): 24–56.

Index